Start a Binge-Worthy Podcast

A Step-By-Step Guide to Creating a Podcast Your
Audience Craves

Krystal Proffitt

Start a Binge-Worthy Podcast: A Step-By-Step Guide to Creating a Podcast Your Audience Craves
by Krystal Proffitt
www.KrystalProffitt.com

For More Info Contact:
support@KrystalProffitt.com
Cover by Thomas McGee
ISBN: 9798650973218

PRAISE FOR
START A BINGE-WORTHY PODCAST

"My only regret is that this book wasn't around when I started my podcast! It would have helped me avoid many failed attempts and hiccups. I love how Krystal breaks down the three key principles of creating a binge-worthy podcast into bite-size pieces so that every aspect of starting, marketing, and launching your podcast is easy to follow, execute, and achieve. If you're a podcast junkie dreaming of creating your own podcast, this book is about to become your bible."

Amy Porterfield, *Entrepreneur &*
Podcast Host of Online Marketing Made Easy

"As a podcast producer myself, I know there are MANY steps you have to take to launch a successful podcast. Start a Binge Worthy Podcast is a must read whether you are looking to launch your own podcast for the first time or you have been in the podcasting space for a while. Krystal breaks it down in an EASY way to remove the overwhelm-- and she does it with a sense of humor! The podcast space is exploding right now, so if you've been wanting to start a

podcast, this book will be your step-by-step roadmap to podcast success!"

Stephanie Judice, *Podcast Management &*
Launch Consultant

"Krystal is your podcast BFF. She's a friend who takes you by the hand to guide you on a journey from to start to launch to create a binge-worthy Podcast you'll love! Krystal's book is insightful, informational, and jam-packed with inspiration!"

Misty Phillip, *Founder of Spark Media & the*
Rocket Podcast Community, Host of the By His
Grace Podcast

This book is dedicated to:
Those brave enough to get behind the mic and share their message with the world.

And also:
Seth Proffitt
Our Boys (Noah, Nicolas, & Neelan)
Nannette Blair
Jesse Blair
Y'all are my foundation. You keep me grounded every single day and remind me to laugh as often as possible.

Free Bonus Content

READ THIS FIRST

You'll see many of podcast episodes, books, videos, resources, and other content referenced throughout the book. You can always go to the website listed below or scan the QR code to take you directly to a resource page with all of the referenced materials.

You'll also find a free bonus training

https://krystalproffitt.com/bookresources/

Make sure you follow me on your favorite social media platforms:

www.Facebook.com/KrystalProffittTx
www.Instagram.com/KrystalProffittTx
www.YouTube.com/c/KrystalProffitt
www.Pinterest.com/KrystalProffittTx
www.LinkedIn.com/in/krystalproffitt/

Start a Binge Worthy Podcast

Start a Binge-Worthy Podcast

A Step-By-Step Guide to Creating a Podcast Your Audience Craves

Start a Binge Worthy Podcast

CONTENTS

Start a Binge Worthy Podcast

INTRODUCTION

"Your accent makes you sound stupid."

I know. Harsh words to say to yourself when you're 18, on your own for the first time, and a freshman in college, but it's really how I felt.

Growing up in a small town in Texas (about an hour and a half east of Dallas) had it perks. The whole "small town living" is a real thing. Community fairs and carnivals were must-attend summer events. The Black-Eyed Pea Festival and the Fiddlers Reunion were something we looked forward to every year. And with a population well below 15,000 people, I never knew that my accent even existed until I left charming ol' Athens, Texas.

But I definitely couldn't hide it when I was out in the real world. "Where are you from? What kind of accent is that? Did you grow up in the backwoods? Dang, you sound like a redneck! Why do you say your I's like that?"

It's easy to look back at those first encounters when I arrived at Texas State University in San Marcos, Texas as immature and silly.

But they hurt.

"I'm from Texas too. I don't understand why I sound different from any of you."

The kids living at Elliott Hall were from all over Texas: San Antonio, Dallas, Fort Worth, Houston, Austin, and other small towns. So why was everyone saying my accent sounded funny? Didn't any of the other students sound like me? That's when first I became aware that my voice was different. Fast forward ten years (and hundreds of podcast episodes later) and my accent making me "sound stupid" is the absolute last thing on my mind. Because let's be real: ain't nobody got time for that!

When it comes to creating a podcast, the most important thing to realize is that your uniqueness – the qualities and the stories that only you have – is what gives you the potential to be a freaking rock star podcaster. Whether you come from a background in business marketing (like me) or a more traditional corporate job or have an accent others make fun of, only you can create the content that's inside of you. My job is to give you the tools to bring out the best in your personality, your expertise, and your experiences in order to impact people with your message - the message *only you* can deliver.

SO, LET'S TALK ABOUT WHAT EXACTLY IS ABOUT TO GO DOWN…

There are three key principles every podcaster must understand: how to start, how to launch, and how to market your show. Throughout the pages of this book, we'll focus on each of these key principles and build your podcast in stages. You can't skip ahead to monetization if you haven't first identified your ideal listener. And you can't properly market your show if you first don't have a podcast someone actually wants to listen to.

In the first few chapters, we'll cover how to start a podcast with the foundational principles that will set the scene for your podcast for years to come. (We're not creating *flash in the pan* podcasts 'round here!) Then, we'll move on to the tactical and technical aspects of the technology you need. (Don't worry, I'm a fan of scrappy over fancy when it comes to the techy stuff.) Somewhere in the middle we'll talk about how to properly launch your podcast so you have listeners ready for you on day one. (You can gain a *ton* of momentum if you launch your podcast the right way!) And finally, I'm going to show you how to market the thing! Because it should come as no surprise that you can't just create amazing content and hope that people will listen to it. (Spoiler alert: the "if you build it, they will come" strategy doesn't work for podcasts!) I'll teach you how to make a great podcast, how to talk about it and attract listeners without feeling icky about it.

And it wouldn't feel right - as your new podcast coach - if we started without this quick, motivational pep talk:

You're going to be terrible in the beginning.

That's okay. This is new for you. You didn't know how to use PowerPoint or Microsoft Word or even Facebook before you learned those programs! You probably weren't good at any of those in the beginning either. So, why would you assume you're going to awesome at podcasting right from the start? I wasn't. You won't be either. But you promise to keep going and get better, right?

Give yourself some grace. Let mistakes happen. Give yourself permission to screw up. Tell yourself, "I can always throw this is the Recycle Bin and start over." But whatever you do, please, please do not give up without giving this an honest try. You got this!

If I can do this, you can too. So, let's do this!

Work with what you have right now, and remember that you can always upgrade in the future. Don't let your podcast setup hold you back from getting started.

Chapter 1: Equipment

CHAPTER 1: EQUIPMENT

"What equipment do I need for my podcast?"
This is the question I see most often from curious new podcasters. And my response is always the same: it depends. It depends on your budget, your ambition, the quality of show you're trying to produce, whether you have enough time to wait on equipment or you need to run out to the nearest store and grab it today, and more. There are many factors when it comes to choosing the right equipment for you and your podcast, but never fear. I came prepared with suggestions.

BASIC NEEDS FOR YOUR PODCAST

As we cover your podcast equipment, we'll talk about your basic needs, optional features and upgrades to consider, my personal microphone recommendations, and your podcast setup. So, to kick us off, what are the basic needs to start your podcast?

1. Computer (with Internet)
2. Quiet Place to Record
3. Microphone

The computer with internet should be pretty self-explanatory, and we'll cover software in depth in a later chapter. So for now, let's go straight to item number two.

QUIET PLACE TO RECORD

There's a *lot* of echo in my office. Like, I've literally tried everything that multiple sound engineers have suggested I try. Curtains over the glass doors and windows. Blankets on the floor. Blankets on the desk when I'm recording. Acoustic panels on the wall. Blanket over my head when I'm recording. (Of all of them, I hated this one the most!)

And that's why I don't record my podcast in my office. I've done as much as I can to get the acoustics just right, but I still record my podcast episodes in my closet from time to time.

I know what you're thinking: "But Krystal, you teach podcasting. Shouldn't you have a fancy studio with all the bells and whistles that you spent hundreds or even thousands of dollars on?"

Um, no. And I don't recommend that for you either.

I encourage people to use what they have, and what does almost every single home anywhere have? A closet. And here's why it's ideal:

- There's a lot of stuff in there. (Clothes, shoes, suitcases, hats, etc.)
- There's carpet—or, if there's not, it's a small enough floor space that's easy to cover with a cheap rug.

In my office, there are tile floors, there's not as much stuff hanging on the walls, and there are windows everywhere. So it's not ideal to record everything in my office.

I want you to find a great space within your home or your office where you can record your podcast with little interruptions and as little echo as possible.

OPTIONAL UPGRADE #1: A DOOR

"What could make this space quieter?" you ask. A door goes a long way in cutting out ambient noise. If you're in a space you can totally control, that's great, and a door may not make a difference. But if your household is anything like mine—I have three kids and a dog—then there's a lot going on all the time. I have all kinds of people going in and out of my house on any given day. But at least my closet has a door!

Another way to cut down on distractions and interruptions is to tell everyone in the house, "Hey, I'm going in here for thirty minutes to an hour. Unless it's an emergency, please don't interrupt. This is really important!" Interruptions and distractions can kill your creative flow or steal your train of thought if you constantly have to hit "pause" when you're recording. If you don't have a door (and even if you do), try to find time to record when you're either alone or have a solid chunk of time where interruptions are at a minimum.

There's something magical about having a dedicated hour or two to record uninterrupted. You can batch all of your podcast content to get several episodes recorded at one time. But it's a lot harder to accomplish that if you don't have a door. Try to find a space where you can just shut people out (with love, of course) and tell them, "This is important. This is my recording space for now."

FERVID OVER FANCY

Please don't get caught up in the idea of trying to have a fancy studio. I get it. Of course, that is the dream. To walk into a fancy studio with beautiful equipment that works properly and has already been tested and set to the correct recording volume, so all you have to do is hit record.

But it's not necessary to get started. Use what you have.

OPTIONAL UPGRADE #2: POP FILTER

Another piece of optional equipment is a pop filter. You've probably seen these on talk shows, images of radio DJs, or footage of a recording artist in the studio. This is a piece of soft, round, mesh-like material that attaches to the microphone. What's the purpose of a pop filter? Well, I'll just give it to you straight: it's a spit catcher. Nope, that's not the technical term. That's what my mom calls it. (Again, we're fervid, not fancy, 'round here.) This piece of equipment is important for catching and deadening the sounds of those puffs of air that come out of your mouth when you say a sound with unintentional added emphasis, like "P" (-puh-), "B" (-buh-), "Ch" (-chah-), "T" (-tuh-), or "Th (-thuh-). If you want to know the technical term, these sounds are called "plosives". (My editor told me that, by the way. I'd never heard the term plosive before. But it's totally appropriate because they sort of explode out of your mouth!)

My pop filter really comes in handy for me. I mean, my name is Proffitt and I talk about Podcasting. It's a lot of mouth noises. If you, too, find yourself making lots of extra sounds when you talk, I suggest investing in a pop filter. It reduces a lot of those noises when you're recording your podcast. Again, this is an optional feature. It's totally not required, but it's a good idea.

OPTIONAL UPGRADE #3: HEADPHONES

"Why do radio DJs and recording artists wear headphones?"

This was a legit question I had when I first started podcasting. But I quickly understood why I needed them when it was time for an interview. First of all, I'd hear feedback from the other person's audio if my mic caught their audio from my speakers, right? But there was something else I hadn't considered when I first started podcasting: my voice volume.

I'm a loud person.

It's the reason my parents picked my voice out of the crowd when I was cheering at a football game. Imagine them walking to find their seats during the first quarter. "Where's Krystal at? We need to sit where we can see—never mind. I hear her. She's closer to the thirty-yard line down there."

When I start talking to my husband first thing in the morning (mind you, I normally have my coffee well before he does), his first reaction is usually a hand gesture that looks like him turning the volume down on my voice. Sometimes he'll say, "You're at a ten. Can you take it down to a three?" I can't help it. I'm naturally a very loud person.

So how do earbuds and headphones play into the picture here? When you have headphones, you can listen to the sound of your own voice when you're recording solo, and you can listen to someone else more easily. I must admit that I don't always use my earbuds when I'm recording solo episodes, but I *always* use them when I'm recording interviews.

For my podcast, I conduct most of my interviews through Zoom. We'll get to that in Chapter 9, but I just want you to make sure that you have all the equipment you're going to need. That way you can *zoom* through the next chapters and be ready for those first interviews. I know you're already eager to get there!

OPTIONAL UPGRADE #4: BOOM ARM

"How can I maximize the space on my desk to podcast?"

This is a piece of equipment that I didn't use until I was well over a hundred episodes into my podcast. But many of my students use these and one in particular said, "It's worked out really great for me. I love that I can literally just push it out of the way when I'm not using it!" And now that I have one too, I 100 percent agree with her!

A boom arm is a piece of equipment that attaches to the edge of your desk and holds your microphone in place. It gives you the ability to swivel your microphone back and forth when you're recording and then push it out of the way when it's not in use. So, if you're tight on space and don't have a lot of room to keep a microphone on your desk at all times, this might be something to look into.

OPTIONAL UPGRADE #5: ACOUSTIC PANELS

"How can I get the best sound in my echoey space?"

As I previously mentioned, I've tried everything to make my office less echoey, and one suggestion from an audio engineer was to try acoustic panels. While the ones I tried didn't work out well for me, I think they are an effective solution for some people.

The cheap ones I purchased did help a little bit, but if you're going to go the route of putting panels on the walls, I'd look into buying thicker, heavier duty ones. If you have the budget and you're able to invest in high-quality acoustic panels, you can definitely create a space for a higher-quality sound.

QUICK NOTE ABOUT SOUND & EQUIPMENT

MICROPHONES

My journey with podcast equipment has taken me from buying a twenty-one-dollar microphone on Amazon to spending hundreds of dollars on one piece of equipment just to test its in-person interview capabilities. I'll share two of my longstanding favorites here, but I want to be very clear on one thing when it comes to microphones: stay within your budget.

There's no need to go into debt for podcast equipment. You can do just fine with the first microphone I used when I got started. I even used it through the first thirty-eight episodes of my podcast and still use it on occasion.

The Fifine USB Microphone was my first mic, and it was so easy. The USB cord plugs directly into the computer and you can start recording immediately. I used it with the pop filter and it worked great.

You can invest lots of money in a fancy microphone and recording equipment, but if you're recording space isn't properly treated to absorb sounds, then your time, money, and efforts will be wasted. It's better to invest your energy in making your space sound better than it is to show off the price tag of your "fancy" microphone.

When I received a one-hundred-dollar Amazon gift card, I upgraded to the Blue Yeti USB microphone. I love the different color choices they offer, and there are more recording options on the Blue Yeti: record yourself, record one-on-one with someone sitting across from you, record with multiple people in the same room, etc. The Blue Yeti has been a great fix for me to get a more crisp, clear sound whenever I'm recording my podcast.

PODCAST SETUP

The last thing I want to cover is your podcast setup. I want to remind you just to keep it simple. Work with what you have right now, and remember that you can always upgrade in the future. Don't let your podcast setup hold you back from getting started.

*Be sure to check the book resources where you can read my suggestions for setting up your podcast equipment and recording in the most optimal room you have in your home or your office.

Krystal Proffitt

Your why is so important! As a podcaster, there will come days when life throws you off track. You'll start asking yourself, "Is my podcast really that important? I'm not seeing the results I'd hoped for. Is it really worth it?"

Chapter 2: Podcast Title & Tagline

CHAPTER 2: PODCAST TITLE AND TAGLINE

"How important is the title of my podcast?"

The title is one of the most important things to focus on when creating your podcast, but it's also not the end-all-be-all. I've changed the name of my podcast, and you can change the name of your podcast if you decide to go in another direction later, too. Just know that it's important, but your podcast isn't dead if you decide to change things up later.

A lot of new podcasters become crippled with decision making. "I have to pick so many things!" I hear the same thing all the time. "What if I pick the wrong title? What if my tagline doesn't work? What if I realize I made the wrong decision?" Again, let's not get bogged down in the idea that once you pick a podcast name, you're married to it forever and ever, amen. No. That's not the case. I'll show you how to pick your podcast title and tagline, but first, let's talk about a few steps that are just as important to consider during this phase of your podcast journey: announcing you're starting a podcast and understanding your "why."

ANNOUNCE YOU'RE STARTING A PODCAST

Before we get started with naming your podcast, there's something to address first: the announcement of your podcast. Did you just have a physical reaction to reading that? Maybe your shoulders got tense, or your stomach got a little tight? I know, it sounds a little premature to talk about announcing your podcast when all we've done is talk about the equipment that you need. We haven't even officially named the thing yet!

But I want you to go ahead and throw the idea out into the world. Why? Because whenever you say it out loud to other people, you're creating an accountability system. You're formally committing to the idea of starting a podcast. And as someone who's worked with many students and clients, I know that putting your podcast out into the world is one of the hardest things to do. Which is why we're going to do it in baby steps.

SIMPLE POST ON SOCIAL MEDIA

Your podcast announcement can be super simple: a social media post that says "I'm starting a podcast this year," with a picture of you and your microphone will do the trick. No one has to know if your podcast is going to launch next week, next month, or on a certain date in the next six months. Your first announcement doesn't need specific dates and times and all that. Yet. I'll show you how to properly launch your podcast later, but planting these little seeds along the way helps your launch be more successful when the time comes. The sooner you talk about it, the longer people know about it.

UNDERSTANDING YOUR WHY

The next thing I want to talk about is understanding your why—the reason you're creating this podcast. Your why is so important! As a podcaster, there will come days when life throws you off track. You'll start asking yourself, "Is my podcast really that important? I'm not seeing the results I'd hoped for. Is it really worth it?"

I have three kids. What does that have to do with my why? I'd like to sit here and give you a noble answer like, "I'm doing all of this for them and the legacy that I'll leave behind." While that is part of my why, the reason I bring up my kids at this particular moment is because kids get sick. Kids have unexpected days off from school during the year. And if I'm not fully committed to the why behind my podcast, I could easily let things slide. "Well, maybe I don't *have* to publish an episode this week. I mean, I was home with two sick kids, and they have a half day on Friday, and my oldest has a project due he really needs help with. Maybe it would be okay to not publish this week..."

Nope. That's not okay. Because we've committed to our podcasts, right? We've said we're going to show up and create this content for our audience so we're going to show up!

MY WHY

My why has transformed over time as I've gone along my journey. Back when my podcast was *The Rookie Life*, it was all about sharing stories of female entrepreneurs. I wanted to inspire and motivate other women. But today, my why looks a little different. While I still aim to inspire and motivate, I'm also dedicated to serving others. I've committed to adding value to the lives of people, just like you, who are wanting to start, launch, and market their podcasts.

So, thank you for showing up here and reading this book. You are my "why," and the reason I keep going even on the days when I want to quit. Even on the days when I'm tired. Even on the days when I really don't feel like it. You are the reason why I keep showing up and keep doing *The Proffitt Podcast*.

NAMING YOUR PODCAST

Do I include my name in the podcast title? Do I use the name of my existing brand or business? There's a lot of confusion around deciding on a podcast name, but I've come to realize there are four things to consider when naming your podcast.

1.Be Specific

Donald Miller's book, *Building a StoryBrand*, may be one of the most influential marketing books I've ever read. But one piece of advice that stands out from everything else in the book is the quote, "If you confuse, you lose." This one statement has helped me create a better podcast, streamline my website, and clean up so much of the clutter that I used to think was necessary in the online marketing space.

You want to be as specific as possible when it comes to how you name your podcast. You *do not* want to confuse people. How can you use keywords, key phrases, or particular industry messaging to name your podcast?

2. Don't Be Cutesy!

A trap I see many online marketers falling into is using cutesy or fancy language when naming their podcast. "But what if the name I thought of is already taken? Can't I look up a few synonyms and use another version of it?" You can, but that's being lazy. There are a lot of fun names that have already been taken, and you do have to make sure that you're not stepping on someone's copyright or trademark, but there are so many more to explore.

Here's a perfect example…

Do you remember in that episode of *Friends* when Joey wrote the letter to the adoption agency? He used fancy, confusing words when he could have kept it simple and to the point. The argument could be made, "He wanted to sound smarter!" But, come on. We know he just ended up confusing everyone with his heart-felt (I mean, aortic-felt) letter.

3. Throw in Your Topic When You Name Your Podcast!

What is the specific topic or industry that your podcast speaks to? Is there a way to throw that name or a synonym to your topic into the title? If you talk about yoga, for example, then make sure you have something related to yoga practices, meditation, or health and fitness. At the very least, include some guiding words that help a listener immediately identify whether your podcast is going to be for them or, more importantly, *not* for them. (Because your podcast won't be for everybody!)

THE SIMPLER THE WORDS, THE BETTER.

If you're talking about finances, use the word "finances" or "money" or another synonym in the title of your podcast. Also, include adjectives or other relevant words to your topic that can identify the kind of value you bring to your audience.

PRO TIP: If you have a few ideas for how to name your podcast, I suggest Googling topics and ideas that revolve around what you want to talk about. See what other phrases and words come up. You never know where the inspiration for your podcast name will spark!

4. Include Your Name Only If It's Relevant!

Another question I get asked all the time is, "Should I include my name in a podcast title?" And my gut reaction is *no*. Unless you're famous or hold some kind of celebrity status, it's not relevant. Obviously, there are exceptions to this, including *The Proffitt Podcast*.

QUICK STORY TIME...

I met my husband in business school. When he first told me that his last name was Proffitt, I didn't believe him! I was thinking, *Here's this guy trying to make himself sound cool so I'll go out with him.* And I was totally wrong. I even made him show me his driver's license because I needed proof that was actually his last name.

But by the time I fell in love with my husband, I'd also fallen in love with and fully embraced the name Proffitt! I mean, come on, it's such a cool name to have in the business world! So that is why I use my name in my podcast. However, it's not that I think I have a certain level of status. It's a fun play on words. And if you have a name that you can use as a play on words, then I say go for it. But if you don't, then I encourage you to find a name that aligns with your topic and the audience you're trying to reach, and maybe includes an emotional word or two that can help people really connect with you.

PRO TIP: Try to keep the name of your podcast short. If you're like me and love to listen to podcasts, then you'll notice most podcasts have pretty short names—between three and five words. This is mainly because you can't fit a lot of text on a podcast logo. My suggestion is to keep your podcast name short and follow up with a killer tagline!

PODCAST TAGLINE

"What is a podcast tagline?"

The way I define it, a podcast tagline is a supportive sentence that helps convey the purpose of your podcast. Because my brain works really well with numbers, systems and processes, I suggest to my clients and students that their podcast tagline has a few distinct words that they use over and over again. Whether it be two to three things that you do, how your podcast solves a problem, or how your podcast adds value to someone's life, choose only a few key points.

PRO TIP: When I was trying to come up with *The Proffitt Podcast* tagline, I started listening to a ton of other podcasts. I examined what their taglines were. I studied what other people were doing. And I noticed that they were using short, single sentences to explain what their podcast does.

After people understand what a podcast tagline is, the natural next question is, "Where does the podcast tagline go?" Well, it varies from podcast to podcast, host to host, and even industry to industry. You can say it at the beginning of every episode. You can include it in a prerecorded clip that you drop into every episode. You can say at the end while you're telling your people you're signing off.

But I recommend that, wherever you put it, your podcast tagline goes into every single episode! Think of it like your mission statement or the tagline of your brand, because that's what it is. The reason for adding your podcast tagline to every episode is branding—a basic foundation of marketing that we'll dig into in a later chapter.

When you find podcasts with great taglines, you'll know. You could probably look at a few of your favorite podcast logos and recite their taglines from memory. They say them in every episode, and you start to associate them with their podcasts. That is the power of an awesome tagline! And that is what you're trying to do with your podcast.

Here is the podcast tagline for The Proffitt Podcast:
Where entrepreneurs go to learn how to start, launch, and market their podcasts.

Again, keep it simple. Don't overthink this. You can always change your podcast tagline later, if you find something else that you would rather use. If the ideas aren't flowing for you right now, that's okay. I think your podcast title is more important. Concentrate on coming up with a great name. The tagline can always come later.

Krystal Proffitt

When you can identify and truly understand your listeners on a deeper level, you're going to connect with them even better.

Chapter 3: Finding Your Ideal Listener

CHAPTER 3: FINDING YOUR IDEAL LISTENER

"I have a great idea for a podcast, but how do I know people will actually listen to my show? And where the heck do I find listeners?"

Finding your ideal listener is so important, and it's one of the things I wish I had spent more time understanding when I first started podcasting. That's precisely why I'm stressing its importance to you here and now!

We're going to talk about identifying and understanding your ideal listener. What does this really mean? This is about creating a persona—the make-believe perfect person that you want to speak directly to every single time you create a podcast episode. I've taken many courses and trainings around understanding your ideal customer, and this persona is usually called your "ideal customer avatar." But, since we're talking about podcasting, we're going to call it our ideal listener. When you can identify and truly understand your listeners on a deeper level, you're going to connect with them even better.

For example, if you listen to *The Proffitt Podcast*, then you know I reference the show *Friends* a lot. I also talk about how much coffee I drink and the fact that I have three kids. The reason I do this is because I know that my ideal listener, maybe that's you, really appreciates this. She gets it. Yes, my ideal listener is a woman. She gets my jokes, and she gets my spunkiness. She understands my enthusiasm for helping others, and she can relate to the piles of laundry in my closet. In exchange for my honesty and vulnerability in connecting with her on a deeper level, she keeps coming back week after week to listen to the new content that I put out.

IDEAL LISTENER ASSIGNMENT

We're going to treat this chapter more like an assignment than the previous ones because it's so important to get this part of your podcast right. (And we haven't even started recording yet!)

Here are a few questions about your ideal audience to consider before we get into actually creating content for your podcast in the next chapter. Feel free to grab a notebook and jot down your answers.

1. Who do you want to listen to your podcast?
2. Where do they hang out online?
3. Do they already listen to podcasts? Or is yours going to be their first one?
4. If they do already listen to podcasts, what do they listen to? Why? What are they doing whenever they're listening to podcasts?

Start thinking about these things now, because it's going to be very important when you start developing content for your podcast. The more you can speak directly to your ideal listener, the faster your podcast is going to resonate with your audience. When that happens, listeners feel like you "get them," and your content gets shared. People start talking about it.

There are a lot more questions and strategies that we can get into, but I can't do the work for you. Only you know your audience. You know who you're trying to speak to. And you know the message they need to hear the most. Set aside some time to devote to getting to know your ideal listener. Don't rush through this. Give him or her a name. What does she do for a living? Does she have kids? Does she work outside the home? Is he struggling to try to bridge the gap between his nine to five and his dream? Is she married? Is he retired? What does she like to do for fun? Does he read books? Which ones? What Netflix shows does she like to binge watch? All the things! Come up with all of this because it matters. It matters so much that you really take the time to get to know your ideal listener so that you can create content specifically for him or her.

Another exercise I want you to try is to journal about who your ideal listener is. I have ideal customer avatars for different aspects of my business, but for the purposes of teaching and sharing in this book, I want to share the persona of the ideal listener for *The Proffitt Podcast*. If you're already a listener of the show, you may see yourself in some of these traits.

IDEAL LISTENER FOR THE PROFFITT PODCAST

Name: Rebecca
Age: 34
Gender: Female
Marital Status: Married, Husband (Steve - 39)
Location: Suburbs of Austin, TX
Household Income: $125,000 annual
Occupation: Life Coach
Kids? Two, Connor, boy-8 and Sophia, girl-4

Principles & Beliefs:
She values her family, her spiritual beliefs, good music, and being understood, and she desires to bring in enough money for her family to get out of debt and start investing for retirement.

Favorite Books, TV Shows, and Podcasts:
Anything by Rachel Hollis, Brene Brown, Elizabeth Gilbert, and the Ramsey Organization. (She's a huge Dave Ramsey nerd!) She listens to all kinds of music

and loves to have dance parties with her family in the kitchen.

Her favorite TV Shows are *Friends, The Office,* and *Grey's Anatomy,* and she can watch any of them on repeat for hours!

The podcasts she looks forward to every single week are *Online Marketing Made Easy* by Amy Porterfield, *Rise* by Rachel Hollis, *The Proffitt Podcast, Why Not Now* by Amy Jo Martin, and *Marketing Your Business* by Stu McLaren.

What does your ideal listener do in their free time?
She enjoys hanging out with her family, going to the movies, being out in nature, having coffee with friends, watching movies at home with the family, reading a good motivational book, working on house projects that make her house feel like home, cooking, and working out.

What is your ideal listener's biggest frustration?
She's frustrated that most people who have a podcast seem to just "have it all together." Like it's a well-oiled machine straight out of the gate. And she doesn't want to raise her hand and ask for help because then she's afraid she'll look like she doesn't know what she's doing. But she really doesn't know what she's doing.

What is your ideal listener's dream?
She'd love to have a podcast that's fun and not
overwhelming. She wants to show up and start
recording with confidence. But she lacks it right now.
She's too tied up thinking she's not an expert in her
field, and it's holding her back from pressing record.

What is your ideal listener's deep, dark secret?
She's embarrassed to do something out of the norm
for her industry. She's worried that people will think
she's stealing their ideas or that she's coming off as a
know-it-all who just likes to talk.

What keeps your ideal listener up at night?
She's worried about making money as a life coach. Is
it really sustainable? Or is she just kidding herself?
She got her first few clients a few months ago, but
new leads aren't showing up the way she hoped they
would. She really wants her family to get out of debt
and pay off Steve's student loans, but she also
doesn't want to deprive her kids of childhood
experiences. She simply wants to make more money.

This may seem like a lot of work to do for your ideal
listener, but this is barely scratching the surface. If you
can understand your ideal listener in an intimate way,
he or she will keep showing up for you every single

week. What do you think I get e-mails, private
messages, and direct messages about most often? Hint:
it's not my podcast content. It's the fact that I shared a
story someone related to. A *Friends* reference, the time I
broke my garage door, or my addiction to ranch
dressing (sad, but very true). These are the things
people relate to, and I intentionally talk about them
because that is what matters. Yes, the core content in
your podcast matters, 100 percent. But if it's all facts
and figures, it's going to be boring. And people don't
subscribe to a show and keep listening if it's boring.

Take the time to really get to know and understand
your ideal listener. Trust me, it's worth it. Especially
when you can bake as much of your personality into
your content as possible so the ideal listeners can relate
to you and become not just ideal listeners, but avid
listeners of your podcast.

It's very important to stay focused and keep planning ahead, because it makes your life so much easier!

Chapter 4: Content Planning and Scheduling

CHAPTER 4: CONTENT PLANNING AND SCHEDULING

"I have about ten good ideas for my podcast. That's it. What am I supposed to do when I run out of those?"

This was one of the most asked questions this past year from clients, students, and the general podcast community. New podcasters are terrified of running out of content ideas. But I have to be honest with you—and don't hate me when I say this—I've *never* had a problem coming up with content ideas. I don't know if it's the way my brain is wired or if I stumbled upon a secret formula. (Don't worry. I'm sharing everything I know here with you! So, if it is a secret formula, you'll know it too.) Let's talk about content planning and scheduling.

BRAINSTORMING PODCAST CONTENT IDEAS

There's a great resource that I tapped into in 2019, and I think it's the reason I never struggle to come up with content ideas. It's a podcast episode I recorded called "Nine Ways to Brainstorm Podcast Content Ideas."

Writing has been in my life since 2014. That's when I owned the title of "writer." This was also around the time I started staying at home full time with my kids. I picked up the hobby of journaling and creative writing, which later led to blogging. I've toyed with writing poetry, children's books, short stories, memoirs, and my first self-published book, *Rookie Devotionals*. You could probably say I've tried it all.

But with all of that creative writing and thinking, there have been some days when I am literally at a loss for words. "What was I talking about here?" I'd ask when I came back to a document I'd been working on less than twenty-four hours before. "This doesn't make any sense. I need to start over. Will anyone else understand this? How can I make this more relatable?" I've been confused, aggravated, and ready to throw a computer across the room. And that didn't change when I started podcasting. The chaos of the ideas (or lack thereof) simply looked a little different.

However, in the midst of creating tons of written content for no reason other than to express myself, I formulated ways to keep the ideas flowing. I'm not saying they're all "great ideas," but the point is, they're ideas. I literally have a free download called "500+ Podcast Ideas for Any Industry," and it only took me an hour or two to come up with. So yeah, I feel like I've tapped into some kind of superpower that I want to share with you today. The "throw the computer against the wall" moments are few and far between these days!

NINE WAYS TO BRAINSTORM PODCAST CONTENT IDEAS

If you're feeling creatively blocked or like you just cannot come up with any more podcast ideas, I want you to go back to these methods over and over and over again. These are the ways I keep my podcast content fresh and keep coming up with ideas that can sustain my content calendar for the entire year.

1. Search Engines

"How to…" is the best way to get started if you're totally blanking. The automatic population of suggested search results on Google and other search engines may be one of the best, simplest tools that we often take for granted. Take your industry, your business, or a topic related to what you do and do a quick Google search. (With this one method alone, you'll come up with more ideas than you could ever use!) If I just type in "How to tie a tie" in any search engine, I'm flooded with ideas: blog posts, YouTube videos, Pinterest pins, images, news-related stories, etc. Take that same "How to" phrase, apply it to something within your industry, and filter out the ideas you'd like to talk about.

You can also search for keywords related to your industry and see what pops up. (You can do that with keywordseverywhere.com, a tool I love to use when I'm trying to come up with new content!) Pay attention to the other search terms that populate. The keywords they use, the titles, the descriptions...all of those may have clues to the next great podcast episode you need to create. If people are already searching for these things, there's a good chance someone out there is looking for the info that you have!

Don't forget to also check the bottom of Google to see "People also searched for" to get ideas. Remember, even if the story has already been told, it hasn't been told by you, from your unique perspective!

2. Whiteboard

Do you remember brainstorming ideas for papers and projects in grade school? If your teacher was anything like mine, she'd have you write a single word on a sheet of paper, circle it, and then draw lines out from the circle. Those lines represented all of the ideas related to the one main topic in the center of the circle.

Well, this method isn't outdated or too childish for brainstorming podcast ideas! For example, for the podcast episode "Nine Ways to Brainstorm Podcast Content Ideas," I wrote the word "Podcasting" on my whiteboard and splintered off tons of lines. I asked myself, "What do you need to podcast? How can you create content? How does publishing content work? What questions do I get asked most often?" And I started filling in any and all ideas that came to mind. One idea in particular I remember podcasters asking me is, "How do you come up with content ideas?" So, I wrote it down. That particular episode was created from a whiteboard brainstorm.

3. Journaling

I already mentioned my writing background, but it's worth noting that you don't have to be a writer in order to use journaling as a brainstorming tool. Journaling can be the same as a whiteboard experience, where you write out one idea and then splinter off everything you can come up with. Except you're just writing everything in a notebook, on a legal pad, or on a plain sheet of paper.

You can also do some free writing, or what I like to call *creative writing*. This is where you imagine someone asking you, "What can you tell me about [Insert your podcast topic]?" And then you answer that question with all of the ideas you can think of!

I rely on this practice when I feel stuck and my other brainstorming tools aren't working. You may feel silly at first, simply writing all the thoughts in your head, but once those ideas start flowing, you won't care! You'll have a full content calendar!

4. Peer Interaction

I meet with an accountability group once a week. I interact with another group often on Facebook messenger. I'm in and out of Facebook groups every single day. I attend a few big conferences related to my audience or the podcast industry once or twice a year. I also attend quarterly in-person events. Peer interactions are priceless!

Whether the people you're interacting with are part of your target podcast audience or not, the questions and topics you'll get from these interactions are so impactful when you sit down to do your next brainstorming session. After I have an interesting conversation or interaction, online or in person, I use this system to brainstorm new ideas:

- If it's appropriate during an in-person conversation, I'll take notes while we're talking.
- Remember the questions people ask and then save them in my Google Drive or the Notes app

on my phone. (You can save Facebook posts directly into your account to look at later.)
- Jot any questions down that would make great podcast episodes after the conversation is over.
- Open a brand-new Google Doc and let the ideas flow.

Take advantage of having like-minded people together in one place. You'll better understand how you can add value to them or other potential listeners.

5. Blogs, Podcasts, YouTube Videos, Magazines, or Online Publications Related to Your Industry

It's likely that you know who the key players are in your industry. So why not take a page from their playbook?
- What are they talking about?
- How can you make the content better?
- Do you agree with them?
- Do you disagree with them?
- Are there any trends happening in your industry?
- Have there been any major shifts in the market?

THIS DOES NOT MEAN COPYING SOMEONE ELSE'S WORK IN ANY WAY!

But it is a way to stay on top of your industry so you can deliver high-quality information to your audience! For example, I listen to many podcasts related to business, marketing, entrepreneurship, social media, and personal development. When I hear about a particular subject that lights me up, I'll take that content I heard, dismantle the pieces that I know my audience would like to hear, and then piece it all together with my own spin.

6. Facebook Groups

Did you know that you can search within a Facebook group for a particular word or phrase? For example, if you're a life coach, you could go into a Facebook group where your ideal audience hangs out and type the words "life coach" or "coaching" or "coach" in the search function to see what pops up. I'll bet you there's a post in there from someone looking for a life coach. Or someone needing recommendations for a life coach. Or a person wanting to know where to find a life coach. Or even someone asking, "What can a life coach do for me?" (You're welcome, life coaches! I just gave you four more podcast ideas!)

What I like to do when I go into Facebook groups where my target audience hangs out is to look up key phrases that I want to create episodes about, find great questions, and save them in my Facebook account so that, when I'm ready to sit down and plan my content calendar, I know I have tons of great topics to discuss on the podcast. Don't underestimate the power of your audience for giving you ideas! (Make sure you join the Proffitt Podcast Online Community Facebook Group so you can collaborate and join others on this podcasting journey.)

7. Survey Your Audience

I've said this on the podcast, to my clients, and students, and I'll say it again here: constantly survey your audience! Like, literally all of the time!

- What do they need help with?
- What could be clearer?
- What makes them happy?
- What frustrates them?
- Where could you expand on a topic?
- What are their basic needs?

And let me tell you, it's easier than ever to do this with social media. You can take a simple poll with the Instagram Stories feature or do a Facebook post with a poll. Or, if you want to go the extra mile, send the occasional survey as a Google Form to your audience. This is 100 percent free and offers you the ability to ask more in-depth questions.

8. Books

Read books related to your niche. Like search engines, there are tons of podcast content ideas flowing through books. You could even create content around what you learned from reading a book, whether it's related to your industry or not! I've done entire podcast episodes about my top books from a given year.

9. A Total Change of Scenery

Sometimes you have to get out of your own way. And that means changing up your environment all together. Take a walk. Workout. Walk the dog. Go to a coffee shop. Go to a library. Take a drive. Take a shower. Just get out of your usual routine and do something different. This is especially true if you feel blocked creatively. The point is to do something out of the ordinary. You'll be surprised what ideas start to pop up when you get out of your comfort zone!

KEYWORDS

We discussed keywords briefly already, but I want to make sure we don't simply skim the surface on them. They are that important, and they will continue to be as podcasts grow in popularity. I wish I had taken the time to really understand keywords when I first started blogging so that, when podcasting came around, I'd already be a pro. But that's not the path I traveled. Now, I have very specific keywords that I use whenever I'm naming podcast episodes, and I'll use in my podcast description, social media posts, and show notes on my website, as well. Keywords need to be baked into every part of your content.

For example, if you have a podcast about life coaching, but all of your episode descriptions are about parenting or your struggles with time management, you're missing the mark. Yes, all of these topics can be related to having an abundant life and achieving work-life balance—two goals of life coaching—but unless you want your podcast to be recognized specifically for parenting and time management, you want to be very careful with overusing those keywords. You can confuse your audience, search engines, and other platforms where your podcast is showing up, because if your keywords are confusing, they won't clearly know what your message is. Make sure you're paying attention to your keywords for your podcast content.

CONTENT CALENDAR

"How do you keep all of your podcast ideas organized?"

Two simple words: content calendar. I was introduced to a simple editorial calendar when I started blogging. It was a basic calendar created in a Microsoft Word Document, and it was blank except for the dates. I'd write in what I wanted to write about each day, and I tried to stick with it. That system didn't work well for me. Now, I have a spreadsheet system in place that has completely changed my content creation strategy, the way I schedule content, and my ability to be consistent! I cannot stress to you enough that if you put these tools and strategies into action now—before you even start recording—you're setting yourself up for success. You're laying the foundation that's going to help you create a consistent podcast that people are going to come back to every single week.

I keep all of my ideas for podcast episodes and the questions that people ask me all of the time in a spreadsheet tab called "content ideas". If I find a good question on Facebook or another social media platform, I put it in that spreadsheet. Then, after a brainstorming session, I'll plug the ideas into my content calendar.

If you're going to create a spreadsheet for your calendar, I advise you to have the following information (example from my content calendar):

Day of Week	Air Date	Topic/Title	Ep. #	Opt-in Freebie	Notes
Tuesday	12/24/19	Podcast Launch Goals, What to Aim For	112	Free 5-Day Podcast Bootcamp	Left "goals" off Launch Episode
Thursday	12/26/19	How Much Does it Cost to Podcast?	113	Free 5-Day Podcast Bootcamp	Basic Needs & Upgraded Options

If something else works better for you, use that. I want you to adjust your calendar to your podcast, your style, and how you work best.

USE BRAINSTORMING & YOUR CALENDAR TOGETHER

Once you've used the brainstorming practices that work best for you, start filling in your content calendar with ideas. I've learned the hard way that it's a lot easier to create and change things in a spreadsheet as opposed to an online calendar. My advice is to keep your online calendar for day-to-day planning and scheduling and have your content calendar live on a separate platform. In other words, don't put all of your podcast episodes on your Google Calendar. It can get messy when you decide to change things up and have to rename and remove episodes.

There are a few specific reasons I want you to have your podcast content planned out before you hit record. Most importantly, it keeps you more organized, and it helps you strategize what content is coming down the road. It's very important to stay focused and keep planning ahead, because it makes your life so much easier!

Krystal Proffitt

I don't like to waste time getting to the point. You're likely to lose someone's attention if you keep talking about why your podcast is amazing and why you're qualified to do this... that...blah, blah, blah. People just want what they came for. So give it to them.

Chapter 5: Podcast Show Format

CHAPTER 5: PODCAST SHOW FORMAT

"Where am I supposed to put my music? And what do I say at the beginning? And what should I say at the end? Should I have prerecorded tracks?"

The podcast show format is one of my favorite things to talk about because this is one way to stand out from the all of the other podcasts.

Do you ever feel like you're having DejaVu when you hear two or three different podcasts within your industry that have the exact same format? You start listening and then think, "Wait have I heard this episode before? Does this person have the same format as she does? Do they have similar music?"

It all starts to blur and feel the same when we all start trying to stick to a standard. Well, I don't believe there is only one specific formula for creating an amazing podcast. I don't want to simply tell you, "Do this, then that, and poof, you'll have a top-rated podcast!" If that's how it worked, don't you think everyone would have a number-one podcast? Instead, let's dive into what actually works: *podcast modeling*.

DEVELOP A PODCAST FORMAT THAT WORKS FOR YOU

Think back to your elementary school days. Remember when you were learning composition and how to write papers? Or how to write a letter? The basic principles of written communication? Can you picture your teacher saying, "Okay, class, when you write something, there is always a beginning, a middle, and an end,"? (I can still picture the old metal desk I used to sit in and the teacher writing with yellow chalk on that green chalkboard that took up the whole classroom. I can still hear the obnoxiously loud pencil sharpener grinding away those shavings on my friend Stephanie's pencil.)

That's how elementary we need to keep the podcast show format. Beginning, middle, and end. You can translate that into podcast terms:

- **Beginning** = Introduction
- **Middle** = Main body of episode (Either solo content or an interview)
- **End** = Outro

Now, let's break down what you need to have in each segment.

Beginning (Intro)

"What should you include in the beginning (or the intro) of your podcast?"

The first thing to consider when you're planning any piece of your podcast is the natural flow of communication. When you meet someone for the first time (let's imagine we're talking about a potential listener), you don't immediately dive into the meat of the conversation. You usually start with some type of greeting or introduction. "Hi, nice to meet you. My name is Krystal. I'd love to chat with you about..."

No matter the format you choose to go with, picture someone listening to your podcast for the very first time. How do you want them to feel when you greet them? Do you want them to know immediately what you're all about? Should you tell them a little bit about who you are? There are no wrong answers here. Just consider what feels right for you and the flow of your podcast.

For me, my intro is technically composed of three microsegments. They are all collectively "the intro," but they include two to three separate pieces of audio.

THE HOOK

The first is the hook. I like to start my podcast with an immediate hook to pull my audience into the episode. I want them ready to listen to everything they're about to hear from the very beginning. I may start with a quick overview of an awesome interview. (Something I enjoy as a podcast listener is to hear other podcasters take a snippet from the actual interview and put it in their intro as the hook. Talk about the ultimate teaser! You're getting a preview of what's to come right out of the gate.) Or I like to tease them with a question I've seen in the podcast community that I know my audience is dying to know the answer to. "How are you supposed to...I've seen this question a lot lately, and today I'm giving you my top tips on how to overcome that. So, let's get right to it!"

MAIN PODCAST THEME

The second microsegment of the intro is what I call the main podcast theme. This is a portion of your podcast (an audio file) that you can prerecord and drop into every episode. It's a segment of the podcast where the same thing is said every single time, and it may include some music in the background. Again, not all podcasts are created equal. Some people like prerecorded intros, some people don't. Not all hosts want to have portions of their show prerecorded. But if you're looking for pieces of your show to automate, this is where I would start.

For example, the main theme of *The Proffitt Podcast* goes a little something like, "Welcome to The Proffitt

Podcast, where entrepreneurs go to learn how to start, launch, and market their podcasts." I include this segment in every episode for one specific reason: brand new listeners. If someone is tuning in for the very first time, then they're probably thinking, "Okay, what are this chick and this podcast all about?" Well, within a few seconds, they'll be able to tell if they want to keep listening, and it lets them self-qualify as someone who should listen to this podcast or not.

SELF-SPONSORED AD OR CALL-TO-ACTION

We'll get really deep into marketing your own products, services, merch, etc. in Chapter 18: Monetization, but I wanted to clue you into the baby step of promoting your own stuff within your podcast. I get a lot of blank stares when I start talking about self-sponsored podcast ads and calls-to-action. I don't know if it's because people have no idea what I'm talking about or if they think I'm crazy for doing them. If you need clear definitions, here they are:

Self-Sponsored Ad: Promoting or plugging your own products, services, events, freebies/opt-ins/lead magnets, tools, and resources within your podcast.

Call-to-Action (CTA): Asking someone to take action, whether it be big or small.

So, if you've ever heard a host on a podcast say, "This episode is sponsored by *my* [fill in the blank]," Then that is a self-sponsored ad. You don't necessarily have to say, "This is my [fill in the blank]." You could say, "This episode is sponsored by [product/service]," and then go into detail how that thing can help your listeners. *If you want to learn more about Self-Sponsored Ads and Calls-to-Action, be sure to complete the Podcast Bootcamp.

"Where do you include the self-sponsored ad?" Well, it depends on what you're promoting. Sometimes I like to put my ads at the very beginning of a podcast episode. I want to make sure my audience knows about what I'm promoting (free or paid), so I put it at the very beginning of my intro. Other times, I'll do my hook, then my main podcast theme, and then my self-sponsored ad. Sometimes I put CTAs within the podcast episode or at the very end. There isn't a rulebook or a mean, old podcast administrator somewhere that's going to give you a slap on the wrist if you do this differently than anyone else. Or even differently than you've done in your own previous episodes. I've changed the format of my podcast multiple times! My best advice is to do what feels right to you and your show.

Middle (Meat of the Episode)

Moving on to the middle or "the meat" of the episode. This is what people came for. This is the most important part of the podcast episode and where you should spend the majority of your time and energy. This is where podcasts tend to vary greatly. Some podcasts are solo shows (where one individual is talking, teaching, giving advice, sharing inspiration, or motivating the audience), and some are interview shows (where two or more people are conversing about a particular topic).

One isn't better than the other. Each style offers a different experience for listeners. I prefer to have both for my podcast, which is why I feel very strongly that people should understand how both are formatted before they decide on which style of show works best for them.

SOLO EPISODES

Whenever I'm doing a solo episode, the intro ends and I go right into what I'm talking about for that episode. I don't like to waste time getting to the point. You're likely to lose someone's attention if you keep talking about why your podcast is amazing and why you're qualified to do this…that…blah, blah, blah. People just want what they came for. So give it to them. (We'll go into more detail in Chapter 8: Solo Episodes.)

INTERVIEW EPISODES

If you're doing a podcast interview, you're going to have a different format. You'll want to do some type of light introduction to the audience of the person you're interviewing. Think about it like you have a friend (your audience) and you want to introduce them to another friend (your guest). This could be as simple as reading the guest's bio and then immediately playing the recorded interview. (More on interviews in Chapter 9: Interviewing.)

End (Outro)

"Finish the story…Wrap it up…Don't leave me hanging." It's so important to wrap up what you're saying! And there are a few ways to end a podcast episode: a simple conclusion, a recap, or a reminder of the number one takeaway you hope your audience got. I like to record my outro last, because I will have already recorded all the other segments and will know what the biggest piece of the episode was and what I want to make sure the audience understands. Here are a few examples of what you can say:

- Simple Conclusion
  - "Well, that does it for this episode…"
  - "That's all for this episode…"
  - "That's it for today, so make sure you go check out the show notes…"
- Recap
  - "Just to recap what we talked about today…"
  - "Here are the [number] things we covered in today's episode…"
- Takeaways
  - "My number one takeaway was…"
  - "I wanted to make sure you understood this one thing…"

When you end your episodes correctly, people have a sense of finality. "Okay, this is over. It's ending. I can move on with my life because I've listened to this awesome podcast episode."

TIME FOR EACH SEGMENT

New podcasters often want to know the timing of everything. (We're a pretty systematic bunch.) If an episode is thirty minutes total, they want to know how much time should be dedicated to each part. I'm not saying that thirty minutes is the magic number for a podcast episode, but for the sake of giving an example, it's what I'm going to use here.

My default timing for a thirty-minute episode is as follows:

- **Intro:** two to four minutes
  - Hook: sixty to ninety seconds
  - Podcast Main Theme: fifteen to forty-five seconds
  - Self-Sponsored Ad/CTA: sixty to ninety seconds
- **Meat of the Episode:** twenty to twenty-five minutes
  - Solo Episode or Interview
- **Outro:** one to two minutes
  - Recap/Takeaway/CTA: one to two minutes

PODCAST MODELING

"How will I know if my show format will work for my podcast topic?"

See what other people in your industry are doing, also known as *podcast modeling*. What does that mean? Well, it's similar to modeling of any other sort. I want you to find a few podcasts that are already successful within your industry, because they are doing something right. And then I want you to pay close attention. I spent almost five years listening to podcasts before I ever created one, and that time served me well. When the time came for me to sit down and plan my podcast show format, I knew the ones that did things really well and the ones that didn't. Find at least three podcasts that you can listen to several episodes of, see what you like about them, see what you don't like about them, and see what you can improve on. Here are some questions to think about as you listen:

- How can I make this better?
- What can I do differently?
- What kind of energy are they bringing to their show?
- What do I love (or not like) about this podcast?

Over the years, I developed my own expectations for what a podcast should be like just by listening to really good and really bad podcasts and asking these questions. Take time developing your podcast show format, but don't overthink it. Remember, you can always change it later if you decide to.

Most podcasters burn out not because the podcast production process is too much or that they don't know what to talk about. Most new podcasters burn out because they spend way too much time editing. And while good audio quality is important for listener retention, it isn't everything.

Chapter 6: Software

CHAPTER 6: SOFTWARE

"The technology is so overwhelming, and I have no idea where to get started...that's why I haven't started."

This is the most common thing I hear in the online world. People are terrified—not just a little nervous, not apprehensive. They are literally *terrified* to learn podcasting software. Why is this? Because it's new. You had to learn how to use Microsoft Word or PowerPoint, and you had to learn how to use Facebook or Instagram! I bet you're on those platforms at least a few times every week, if not daily!

You can learn podcast software. Now, repeat after me, "I can learn podcast software." I say this to my students and clients all the time, and I'm going to tell you too: *If I can do this, you can do this!* I don't have any special degree, certificate, or training in audio software. I didn't even know how to use half the apps on my iPhone until my kids showed me how! So, don't tell yourself you can't handle the software part of podcasting.

Besides, look at us.

Here we are, on chapter 6 of a podcasting book, and this is the first time we've even talked about the actual recording of your podcast. Do you see what I'm trying to say? The technology is only a small portion of the process. It's only one piece of the puzzle. And quite honestly, it's where I see too many people wasting their time. I'm probably going to get in trouble for saying this, but this is my book and I can say what I truly believe here, so I'll say it: the software isn't that important.

Hear me out. Don't worry, I'm still going to give you tips and strategies for working with podcast software, and I have tons of podcast episodes and YouTube tutorials about podcast editing, but it's important to understand my mindset behind podcasting so you see why I do things the way that I do.

I'm a mom of three boys. I work out of my home. I travel a few times a year to see family and go on vacations. I do not have a million-dollar recording studio or thousands of dollars' worth of podcast equipment. (Remember when I told you I got started with a twenty-one-dollar microphone I bought off Amazon?) With that being said, I like to experiment. Instead of limiting myself into believing the only way I can record my podcast is in a studio with perfect sound, I play around with different recording techniques.

I've recorded in my echoey office with my affordable microphone, at a conference with 800-plus people in the background using my handheld recorder, in a hotel lobby using the voice memos app on my phone, and in my closet with my laptop and fancy microphone. I've used many setups and software applications in the process, and I can't say any single one of them is the only one to use. Typically, I use what works for me that week. If we're out of town and I have to record, I'll take my handheld recorder or use my phone. If it's a typical week, I may record in my office.

The point is to be flexible. If you have it in your head that you can only record when the environment is perfect, I'm afraid you'll get discouraged at some point along the way when life throws you a curveball—which will inevitably happen.

Recommended Software

Let's talk about the software basics you need to know in order to record your podcast. Obviously, a walk-through, step-by-step tutorial would be incredible to include here, but like I said, there are many online tutorials and examples you can use to brush up your skills. I've linked to several in the Podcast Bootcamp, and there are more on my YouTube channel. But I can share with you the software I recommend.

AUDACITY

This is the audio editing software I use, and I recommend it to my students and clients. I've used it since day one. I have a PC and it's been a great software for my podcast.

GARAGEBAND

This is the software that comes standard on most Apple products. (It can be used on newer models of the iPhone as well.)

As of the publishing of this book, Audacity & GarageBand are both free programs.

HINDENBURG JOURNALIST

This is the latest digital audio workstation that I've been experimenting with in the last six months. It is a paid software, but doesn't require a monthly subscription at the time of this book publication. It's worth checking out if you want an option that's easy to use and offers settings that other programs do not.

ADOBE AUDITION

If you're wanting to get more advanced and technical with your podcast, then Audition is a great option. While I don't use this program for my podcast, it comes highly recommended by audio engineers in the industry.

Podcast Software Basics

Most podcasters burn out not because the podcast production process is too much or that they don't know what to talk about. Most new podcasters burn out because they spend way too much time editing. And while good audio quality is important for listener retention, it isn't everything.

Here are the important basic functions you'll need to know in order to use your podcast editing software successfully. (Note that the terms below are associated with the functions inside of Audacity. Names vary by program and version, but the functions, themselves, should be consistent.)

- **Recording & Playback**
  - When you open Audacity, you can see that there is a bright red button at the top left. This is the Record button. This is the button you'll press whenever you're ready to record a solo podcast, intro, outro, interviewee bio, self-sponsored ad, call-to-action, or anything else you need to say in your podcast.
  - Just hit the Record button, "Say what you need to say" (Do you hear John Mayer's voice in the background?), then hit the Stop button whenever you're done.

- ○ The finished product is an audio file. When you want to listen to the audio you just recorded, simply hit Skip to Start (left-facing arrow button with a bar) and then press the green Play button. You should hear the exact message you just recorded. Try it, and see how it sounds!
- **Selection Tool**
  - ○ This is the tool you use to navigate to different sections of your podcast episode. It looks like a cursor you'd find in just about any text box. If you need to listen to the audio from a certain point within your file, use the Selection Tool to pick your place, then hit Play. You can also use the Selection Tool to grab areas of audio you need to delete, cut and paste, or make any number of other adjustments to.
- **Cutting & Deleting**
  - ○ There are times when you'll mess up. You'll let out a long, drawn-out "Ummm" when you forget your train of thought, or you'll sneeze or grossly clear your throat or bang your knee on the desk, or your dog will bark, or the lawn guys next door will start weed eating while you're recording...

- o Trust me, there are many reasons for cutting and deleting sections of the audio out of your recording. Don't let those little mistakes trip you up.
- o I don't do as much "editing out" now as I did at the beginning of my podcast. It takes a lot of time to do, and I find that my audience enjoys a rougher, raw episode more than a perfectly polished one. But that is also the premise behind *The Proffitt Podcast*. My motto is, "Keep it up. We all have to start somewhere!"

- **Time Shift Tool**
  - o This is the tool with the double arrows, and you'll use it to drag your audio files to just the right spot. This tool allows you to slide an audio track back and forth, and you can use it to align tracks end to end, match up your voice with where you want music to fade in, or adjust when you want an audio file to start. If you have music that needs to be played before the episode intro, then you'll use the Time Shift Tool to move the music to the point where you need it to be within the episode.

- **Recording Volume Adjustment**
  - As I mentioned earlier, I'm a very loud person! (Ask my husband if you don't believe me. Especially after my second cup of coffee in the morning!) I have always been loud. I will always be loud. So instead of trying to change myself for my podcast, I simply adjust my surroundings and my recording volume whenever I'm producing my podcast.
  - In order to do this, slide the recording volume scale to 50 to 60 percent of the total volume. I could probably go lower, because I really am *that* loud, but I find that range usually works for me. Any lower than that and I have to turn the volume way up when I listen to the playback. Any higher than that and I'm in the dreaded "red zone."
- **Saving**
  - This should be a familiar process if you've created other files on similar programs, but for the sake of teaching, we're going to pretend you haven't.
  - Go to File, Save or Save As, find the appropriate folder or create a new one,

and name your audio file according to how you set up your show.

- Maintaining organization for your audio files is super important, especially the more podcast episodes you create over time! For example, I create an intro file for each episode, and I name it "Episode # – Intro." This becomes important when you start importing and exporting audio files. You want to make sure you're grabbing the right clip for the right episode.
- PRO TIP: Take some time and create a file system to guide how you will name your podcast episodes and all of the components that go into them.

- **Importing**
  - Many times, you'll need to Import different files into Audacity. These could include prerecorded interviews, music, self-sponsored ads, intros, outros, etc. You'll need to import all of those separate files into the episode you're working on.
  - You can select multiple files at one time to import, but I recommend importing files in the order that they'll appear in that episode. For example, you don't want to have the outro and the outro music

imported at the beginning of your episode. This makes more work for you in the overall process.

- **Exporting**
  - In order to upload your audio file from Audacity into your online podcast hosting site, you must Export it as either an MP3 or WAV file.
  - Your hosting site will not accept raw files from your recording software (i.e. Audacity files). It *must* be saved as an MP3 or WAV file before it's uploaded.
- **Effects**
  - There's an overwhelming feeling that sets in when you open the Effect option in Audacity and see how many options there are, but don't let that discourage you. I know there are probably a million different ways to use the different kinds of effects available within the program, but I only use one. Yes, you read that right—one. I use the Adjustable Fade effect within Audacity to have my music slowly fade in during my intro and my outro. I want it to be a subtle entrance and not a loud disruption.

- **Zoom In and Zoom Out**
  - When I first started podcasting, I had no idea why anyone would ever use the Zoom In and Zoom Out tools. It wasn't until I started editing a lot of my episodes that I realized I could hone in on the exact part I needed to edit out with the Zoom In tool. You can pinpoint the exact moment when you subtly coughed, grab it, and cut it easily when you zoom in.
  - It works exactly how it sounds. You place the Selection Tool exactly where you want to see the audio closer and click the Zoom In button. The audio will get closer (shown in faster increments), and you will be able to see more detail. The more you click Zoom In, the quicker time will go. If you find yourself looking at nanoseconds of audio, you probably went in *too close*. Simply click the Zoom Out button to get readjusted to a normal playback increment.

Make sure you check out the Audacity videos on the book resources page.

Over-Editing is the Silent Killer

If I could wave a magic wand and make all new podcasters feel more confident with their podcasts, I'd give them the ability to hear their own voices with potential and clarity rather than criticism and doubt. If you're brand new to the podcast game, you're not going to be any good at first. Oh, whoops. I said that wrong. I was supposed to preface with, "I've got some good news and some bad news…" But, spoiler alert, that's the bad news! You won't be a shining star the first time you turn on your microphone. The good news is that you *will* get better over time.

"Yeah, but I don't sound professional when I say 'um' or pause too long or take a deep breath. I need to edit all of that out to sound legit, right?" Nope. No. Ain't nobody got time for that! You see, every minute you spend over-editing your audio to sound "perfect" is a minute you could have spent creating a new piece of content. Or marketing an existing piece of content. Or researching the next amazing topic you'll deliver to your audience. Or engaging with your audience online. Or finding the next guest that'll absolutely blow their minds!

So no, I don't think you need to edit out every, single little detail that isn't perfect. Perfection is overrated. Plus, we have too many people sounding like robots these days. I relish in the moments where I mess up and have the opportunity to tell my audience I messed up. And they love it too. How do I know? Because they tell me. They love it when I can laugh at my inability to mash two words together. "Blag past...nope, blog post. But I guess you can call it a blag past. It's actually a blog post for a podcast...no that's, dumb." If I had edited that part out, I would've missed the opportunity to connect with the people in my audience who are worried about saying the wrong thing. It's okay to say the wrong thing and laugh at yourself. It's like giving someone permission to be themselves.

If you need permission, there. I just gave it to you. "I give you, [INSERT NAME], permission to mess up and be yourself on your podcast."

...if you're feeling that imposter syndrome creeping in to tell you, "Oh, I don't really know. Who am I to tell other people something on this podcast?"

What you're feeling is a real thing. And it does feel a little weird when you're first getting started with your podcast. So, I want to give you all the tools I can to help you be successful with the first episode of your podcast.

Chapter 7: Record Your First Episode

CHAPTER 7: RECORD YOUR FIRST EPISODE

"How will I know when I'm ready to start recording?" Well, now, if you've read everything else up to this point, you're ready to start recording your podcast. We've already covered what you need to get started: equipment, podcast title and tagline, your ideal listener, content creation, podcast show format, and recording basics. I promise, you're ready.

SETTING UP YOUR PODCAST FILES

We briefly touched on podcast files in the last chapter when we discussed Exporting, but let's talk about them in more detail now. What do I mean by setting up your podcast files? Well, to keep it simple, I mean keeping your podcast files organized. Knowing where your files are and being organized is vital to success when it comes to podcasting.

Pretty soon, you'll have audio files that are full episodes as well as intros, outros, music, ads, interviews, CTAs, and all the other types of content files you could possibly include in your podcast. It's overwhelming (and super frustrating) if you're looking for a particular file and you cannot find it anywhere. I want to make sure that you set yourself up for success *before* you ever start recording and have so many audio files all over the place that you can't find what you're looking for.

And since I'm so passionate about naming my files, I thought I'd give you a tour of what my folder and file naming system looks like. You can either take this and run with it or come up with a filing system that works for you. This file system is setup on my computer hard drive, but it can easily be translated to a cloud-based file system.

FILE FOLDER SYSTEM FOR
THE PROFFITT PODCAST

- The Proffitt Podcast
  - All Episodes
    - "All Episodes" is the folder for files that are going to go into every single episode. Whether it's your main podcast theme, your outro, CTAs, music, or self-sponsored ads, create this folder for anything that needs to be dropped into each episode.
    - When you're in your audio editing software, you can import all of these files at one time, so you won't have to

waste time going in and out of folders looking for everything. Trust me, it's a huge time saver to have everything in one place, grab the files you need, and drop them into your podcast episode.
- PRO TIP: Having all the necessary prerecorded clips in this folder can help speed up the editing process.
○ Episodes
- The "Episodes" folder is where I keep a subfolder for every single podcast episode. As time has gone on, I've archived past episodes to keep the folder visually decluttered. There are folders within this folder for "Episodes 000-049" and for "Episode 050-100," as well as subfolders for every single podcast episode containing the unique intros, outros, and any other relevant content. Within the "Episodes" folder, I've categorized each subfolder as Episode ## - Name of Episode (For example, "Episode 056 - Sound Like a Pro, Even When You're Not"). It's really helped because it's kept everything in one place.

- **SOLO EPISODES:** When you click on each subfolder, you'll find the Audacity files associated for the episode as well as the final MP3 or WAV files I've uploaded into my podcast hosting site, Buzzsprout. (More on podcast hosting sites in chapter 13!)
- **INTERVIEW EPISODES:** As you can imagine, there are many more pieces to an interview episode. Whether you're collecting a headshot from your guest, their bio, the actual interview, or any other files for the interview, you want to keep them all in one place.
- Regardless of how you name your podcast episodes, have a system in place that works for you. You don't want random files that are labeled "1, 2, 3" or something equally confusing. Maybe you want to hire someone to help you with your podcast. But what if you can't even navigate your own files? Come up with a system that makes sense for you and your podcast team.

- Podcast Show Guidelines
    - This folder contains the guidelines we'll talk more about when we get to chapter 9. Again, I want to be able to find them when I need them to e-mail them to a guest.
- Music
    - The "Music" folder is for any tracks related to my podcast music. We'll dive more into what kind of music files you can have for your podcast in chapter 10, but just know it's important that your podcast music has its own folder.
- Self-Sponsored Ads
    - The "Self-Sponsored Ads" folder is where you'll keep all the prerecorded promos you want in your episodes. Different from the "All Episodes" folder, you'll have every ad you want to include over the life of your podcast here. We'll dive more into this in the marketing section of the book, but I do want to mention it here because if self-sponsored ads are something you want to use (to grow your e-mail list, or promote lead magnets or other free

resources that you want to send to your audience) then you want to keep them separate from your other files.
- ○ Podcast Main Theme
  - ■ While the Podcast Main Theme is also in the "All Episodes" folder, I've changed it a few times over the life of my podcast. Keeping a separate folder for iterations of the main theme just made sense for my podcast.
- ○ Additional Folder Options to Consider
  - ■ Logos and Images
  - ■ Branded Artwork (Graphics)
  - ■ Video Files

I know podcast file organization isn't sexy, but you'll be glad you spent the time setting up a system before you're hundreds of episodes in and you've accidentally saved an audio file in the wrong folder. (I speak from experience on this one!)

PODCAST TRAILER EPISODE

While your podcast trailer isn't technically your first piece of podcast content, it's still very important. This is the audio track you'll use to connect your podcast to your hosting site (which we'll discuss in further detail in chapter 13). Podcast trailer episodes vary from show to show, but when it comes down to it, the purpose of it is simple: to get your show connected to all of the podcast directories, including Apple Podcasts, Google Play, Spotify, and others.

WHAT NEEDS TO BE IN YOUR PODCAST TRAILER?

While not all podcast trailers are created equal, most of them have the same basic information: the name of the podcast, a little about the host(s), the podcast launch date, what value the podcast will provide for listeners, and how often episodes will be published.

HOW LONG DOES THE TRAILER NEED TO BE?

This really depends. I've seen podcast trailers that are barely thirty seconds and others that are over thirty minutes. It just depends on you, your show, the content, and what is most important for your audience to know before you actually launch.

DOES THE PODCAST TRAILER COUNT AS MY FIRST EPISODE?

Yes, and no. Yes, it is the audio track you'll use to connect your podcast to your hosting site before you technically "launch." But no, you don't have to keep it as an official podcast episode after your show goes public if you don't want to.

I uploaded a new trailer episode to my podcast after I rebranded. I never went back and changed the intros and outros to my old episodes of *The Rookie Life* because, well, I didn't think I needed to. It seemed like a huge waste of time to go back and make everything appear "perfect." So instead, I recorded a new Episode 0 that explains the transition from the first forty-four episodes of the podcast to *The Proffitt Podcast*. But for the purposes of recording, you can create the trailer episode first.

Recording Your First Podcast Episode

Okay, I feel like we're starting to procrastinate, and I don't want to waste another moment. I want you to start recording your first podcast episode. Look back over the notes about your podcast software, your show format, and how to develop your podcast content.

If you're feeling a little squirmy, make sure you listen to "Episode 59: Sound Like a Pro, Even When You're Not." I really want you to go listen to this episode if you're feeling that imposter syndrome creeping in to tell you, "Oh, I don't really know. Who am I to tell other people something on this podcast?" What you're feeling is a real thing. And it does feel a little weird when you're first getting started with your podcast. So, I want to give you all the tools I can to help you be successful with the first episode of your podcast.

There's nothing more for me to say here except that you can do this. You can take that energy of being scared but excited, a little nauseous, and terrified to create your first podcast episode. I believe in you.

Now, go hit Record!

You're not perfect.
I'm not perfect.
I wasn't perfect when I started,
and I'm still not perfect today.
But the more you start
recording yourself, the faster
you'll feel comfortable and more
confident.

Chapter 8: Solo Episodes

CHAPTER 8: SOLO EPISODES

"Should I create solo episodes or interviews for my podcast?"

My answer is both. It's great to give yourself options by creating a mixed podcast. But before we jump the gun and get too deep into all the ways to podcast, I want to focus on solo episodes. Let's talk about what to say during a solo episode and then how to use your content calendar to pick the first few solo episodes of your podcast.

Enter Solo Episodes

Quick story time...

I truly believed I would *never* record solo episodes. "I always want to have interviews and offer tons of value by bringing on experts in my industry," I kept telling myself as I planned out the beginning stages of my podcast. "And that's just how everything is going to be. Forever and ever. Amen." (Boy, was I in la-la land thinking everything would always turn out exactly how I planned!)

As you can probably guess, that's not how things worked out. Life happened, and something came up—as it always does. I encountered a technical glitch that prevented me from recording two months' worth of interview episodes. It was heartbreaking. And to be perfectly honest, it scared me.

"Am I cut out to do this? Who am I to keep trying to figure this podcast stuff out? What am I even doing? Is this all really worth it?"

This "technical glitch" happened during the first few months of my podcast and, well, it ended up being kind of a miracle. Don't get me wrong. I'm not happy that I lost two incredibly amazing interviews—one with a dear friend of mine who shared lots of stories about her own beautiful journey. The miracle was teaching me not to rely on looking outside myself anymore. The miracle was me realizing that I—me, by myself—had lots of value to offer. I have so many relatable stories and experiences that I could share with my audience. These stories add a ton of value without having an expert guest on the show. And I'd be willing to bet you have these stories, too.

Another part of the miracle was the burden that solo shows lifted off my content calendar. No longer was I reliant on someone else's schedule to make the podcast work. No more wondering, "What if something comes up? What if someone cancels or a kid gets sick? What if there's another no-show?"

There are a lot of unpredictable things that can happen when you rely on other people's schedules to fall directly in line with your own. Solo podcast episodes are a great way to keep your content calendar filled throughout the year while also giving tremendous value to your audience.

WHAT GOES INTO A SOLO EPISODE?

Here are a few key things you need to create solo episodes for your podcast:

- Personal Stories
  - Storytelling seems to be a natural trait for most podcasters, whether it's their ability to talk about their own lives and experiences, or turn a somewhat boring detail into a story that makes you hang on their every word. Personal stories are the perfect way to quickly become relatable and trustworthy with your audience. Even if you don't know it yet, you have so much value to offer them, and stories are a great way to do it.
- Resources and Recommendations
  - The online resources that you have or use can be repurposed into solo podcast episodes. Let's say you created a free resource for your ideal listener that you're already delivering on your website. You could talk about the meaning behind that

resource, why you created it in the first place, the benefits it offers, and a brief overview of what it is and who it's for.

- ○ What are some other ways that you can repurpose content you already have and turn it into a solo podcast episode? You don't have to reinvent the wheel. Look around at some of the resources you've already created and see what you can do to turn those into solo podcast episodes.
- Advice and Tips
    - ○ The next thing to consider is offering tactical advice and tips for your audience. What do I mean by that? If you have a podcast that is formatted around teaching your audience something, then make sure they walk away from a solo episode with strategic action items. For example, I like to provide strategies, tips, or key takeaways in my solo podcast episodes.

The more you practice with solo podcast episodes, the easier it will be to make conversations flow more naturally whenever you're doing an interview with someone else.

CHOOSING YOUR FIRST FIVE SOLO EPISODES

Now, we're going to pretend you've already recorded your very first podcast episode, even if you haven't yet. (Maybe you're waiting to finish this book and then take action. That's cool. And if that's you, we're also going to pretend you've done everything in the book up to this point.)

By now, you should feel comfortable with the content ideas that you've created. You've had some practice rounds with your recording software, and I know you're ready to go! I want you to go record your first five solo episodes. *GASP!* Hang on - before you have a full-on panic attack, let me explain something very important. That doesn't mean these episodes are getting published. Or that anyone else ever has to hear them. You're not putting these out into the world quite yet.

I just want you to get comfortable behind the microphone, make some mistakes, and get them out of your way now. Because mistakes are going to happen. Let me say it in another way: mistakes are *definitely* going to happen. I 100 percent guarantee it! You're not perfect. I'm not perfect. I wasn't perfect when I started, and I'm still not perfect today. But the more you start recording yourself, the faster you'll feel comfortable and more confident. And don't worry, you're going to get better as time goes on. So, I want you to take your content calendar and your content ideas, and pick five solo episodes that you want to be the first ones.

PRO TIP: Remember, you can always move these episodes around. Even if you record them back to back to back, you can shift them within your calendar to whatever schedule works best for you. Maybe you have an idea and all of a sudden, you're like, "Oh, man! My audience needs to hear this one before they hear this other one." Not a problem. You can always switch them around, even when the content is ready to go. You haven't uploaded your episodes anywhere yet (we'll get to that in chapter 13). All you've done at this point is created audio files for your ideal listener using the content ideas and podcast format you've already set up. They'll simply be files saved on your computer. You can still make changes at any point.

Here is your next assignment: pick five solo podcast ideas, record those five episodes, and celebrate how far ahead of the game you are! And we haven't even talked about launching the podcast yet.

Krystal Proffitt

Podcast interviews are definitely a skill…

…just know when you're getting started that the process may feel a little clunky at first.

Don't sweat it! You'll be better on your tenth interview than you were on your first!

Chapter 9: Interviewing

CHAPTER 9: INTERVIEWING

"How can I add different points of views to my podcast and make it a more engaged, dynamic show for my audience?"

ENTER INTERVIEWS

While I know some podcasts can survive solely with interviews or solo episodes, I still think it's great to offer your listeners a variety of content. Interviews keep things interesting, and guests can bring fresh perspectives on topics you may have already covered in your solo episodes. Plus, from a listener perspective, you feel like you're getting behind-the-scenes access to conversations you'd otherwise never hear. (That's why I personally love listening to interviews with my favorite thought leaders, celebrities, and comedians!)

Now, we have a lot to cover for interviews. Not only does adding a guest into the episode mix make your podcast more dynamic, but it also adds a layer of tasks and considerations to juggle. In this chapter, we're going to cover the interview basics, how to find potential guests, what software to use to schedule guest interviews, how to create podcast show guidelines, how to set up an interview, what to do with the audio after you've recorded, and how to navigate the interview thought process. I know, that sounds like a whole lot of information. It is. The good news is that I'm going to break it up into digestible sections so you can focus on one thing at a time. There are some very strategic pieces that you need to understand and apply correctly in order to create a great experience for you and your guests.

Interview Basics

Let's talk about who you should bring on to your podcast as a guest. Whether the person you're looking for is another expert in your industry, a well-known author, or someone wanting to promote their product or service, I highly recommend you have a litmus test in place for determining who qualifies as a guest. What does that mean? That means finding people who align with the principles and values of your podcast. This really hits home for me. I've had people reach out to me who are interested in being on my podcast only to find out the product they'd like to promote does *not* align with me, my audience, or my overall message. One of these people shared a very weird, awkward pitch. When I received it…well, let's just say it was a cringe-worthy moment.

In my gut I knew that if I took this interview and let them promote their product on the podcast, I wouldn't be able to sleep at night. I know that sounds dramatic, but that's how clearly I knew that their pitch didn't align with my podcast. So, go with your gut whenever you're choosing someone to be on your podcast. If it doesn't feel right, it's okay to say no. Do not feel like you have to accept any guest that says they want to be on your podcast, even if you're just starting out. It's better to have solo episodes for a while than to interview people who don't align with your goals.

How to Find Potential Guests for Your Show

How do you find potential guests for your show? This is going to vary from industry to industry, business to business, and podcast to podcast. I want to share with you the things that I have found work really well for finding quality people to bring onto my podcast.

The first is asking your friends, family, and others in your immediate network. I filled up the first few weeks of my podcast content calendar with people I knew and friends of friends. I told several of my friends, "Hey, I'm starting a podcast…This is what I'm doing…This is what I'm thinking…These are the types of people I'm looking for…Do you have anybody in this industry?"

And honestly, I was a little overwhelmed by people that raised their hands and said, "I would love to be on your podcast!" And several friends who weren't a fit themselves told me, "I know someone that would be perfect for this!" Don't be afraid to reach out to your immediate network. You may ask them and they say no. That's okay. At least you have a place to start that doesn't feel as scary as e-mailing complete strangers. Use your connections. Ask your friends and family. And be sure to tell them exactly what type of guests that you're looking for.

Who Do You Want to Interview?

This brings me to my next point: you always want to know who you *want* to interview. You don't have to have a specific profile with detailed criteria like, "They need to have had [X] years of industry experience, have done [Y] particular job, and been successful at [Z]." It doesn't have to be that at all. However, you do need to set some boundaries around who you want to come on to your show and, more importantly, who you don't. Otherwise, the quality of the interviews (and your podcast) could go downhill very quickly. At the very least, set a few basic guidelines for who you want to have on your podcast.

For *The Proffitt Podcast*, guests have to meet at least one the following criteria:

- Help entrepreneurs with some aspect of their business

- Know a specific area of the podcast industry and be able to share something from their perspective
- Offer advice for podcasters in the start, launch, and market stages

How to Schedule Guest Interviews

When I started doing podcast interviews, there were a lot of back-and-forth messages with my guests. It usually looked something like this:

Me: *"Here are my available dates. Choose a time slot that works for you."*
Guest: *"Oh, those days and times don't work for me. How about Monday at 6:00 pm instead?"*
Me: *"I can't do that because it's right in the middle of dinner. How about Thursday at noon?"*
Guest: *"Thursday is no good for me because I have an appointment at 12:30. What about…"*

This conversation happened all the time when I first started doing podcast interviews. And I was *super frustrated* with the process. (I imagine my interviewees weren't thrilled with the cumbersome scheduling either.)

Now, I use a scheduling tool called Calendly to schedule guest interviews. As of the printing of this book, Calendly is a scheduling software that integrates with Google Calendar. It takes all the back and forth out of scheduling, and it's perfect for people, like me, who don't have a team member devoted to helping me schedule podcast interviews. And I absolutely love this platform.

It's as simple setting up your calendar with the dates and times you want to take interviews, which helps set up healthy time boundaries around your podcast. Then, you integrate your Google Calendar to reflect the appointments you already have on your schedule so you don't overbook yourself. (Think doctor appointments, other meetings, or your son's school party.) As long as you have that time marked "Busy" on your Google calendar, this scheduling tool works within the parameters of the timeslots you designate. Then, you just send your guests the Calendly link, and they pick the time that works for them. No more back and forth! You can even collect data like your podcast guest's bio and links they want to share on the show, so you can have all of their information in one place.

Once you've configured the initial setup of what days and times you want to schedule interviews, the rest is easy. Simply copy the URL of your scheduled event ("podcast interviews") and send it to your guest via e-mail, Facebook Messenger, Direct Message on

Instagram, or however you are chatting with potential guests.

Podcast Show Guidelines

"What if someone who's going to guest on my podcast has never been on a podcast. Don't I need to tell them how it all works?"

Yes, you do. As a gracious host, you don't want to leave your guests scouring the Internet to find videos related to how a podcast interview works. You want to be proactive, prepared, and helpful for your guests. That's where your podcast show guidelines come into the picture.

I've been a guest on many podcasts, and the ones that I'm most excited to show up for have laid out their entire podcast interview process for me, because it can vary greatly from show to show. These guidelines are in place for guests who are brand new to podcast interviews, have asked for specific instructions, or have asked, "Is there anything I need to know before our interview?"

The last thing you want your guests to see is a podcast host that seems to just throw everything together, looking completely frazzled, and appearing disorganized. Your podcast show guidelines are a way to show that you're a legitimate podcast host and you're serious about what you're doing.

WHAT ARE PODCAST SHOW GUIDELINES?

Your podcast show guidelines are a tool for you to prepare your guests for their interviews and answer some of the common questions guests have about interviews:

- What is the format of the show?
    - Will you be interviewing them alone? With a cohost?
    - Do you send them questions ahead of time?
    - Will there be a segment of the interview where they can plug their business/services/etc.?
- How long will the interview be?
    - How long does the entire process take?
    - Should they set aside an hour or two for the entire process? Or will it only take twenty minutes?
- Give guests the opportunity to ask questions before the interview.
    - People don't often know they have questions until they're prompted with words that answer their subconscious thoughts. "Oh yeah, I was thinking about that," was the response I had when I read

the guest posting guidelines for a blog I once wrote for.

- The goal is to eliminate all uneasiness your guests may have so they feel comfortable well before your interview. Part of that is letting them know, "It's okay to mess up. Here's what happens if we do…"

  - There's a section in my podcast show guidelines where I let the guest know it's totally okay if they screw up! I understand that other podcast hosts may not give their guests that kind of warning, but I live and work in an environment I can't always control. If I was going to be a guest on someone's podcast and the host said, "Hey, it's totally fine if your kid busts into the room screaming because they have a poopy diaper or your dog starts barking or your doorbell rings. I get it…that's life! We can totally edit those things out!" I'd feel a lot better about the whole thing. So, that's what I tell my podcast guests.

Not taking the entire interview too seriously helps them ease up a little bit and get comfortable. Remember, the goal is to eliminate uneasiness for your guest. Come on, let's be good hosts.

How to Set Up a Podcast Interview

"Okay, I'm with you. But how do I set up the technical aspects of a podcast interview?"

I see lots of new podcasters hesitant to do interviews in the beginning because they're terrified they're going to do it wrong. "It looks complicated...I'm not techy enough...I don't know how to set everything up or which programs to use." I've heard all of the excuses. And that's what they are: *excuses*.

Now, you may be saying, "No, wait. I really don't know how to set up a podcast interview." But after you read this, you won't have that excuse anymore. (See what I did there?)

SET AN INTENTION FOR THE INTERVIEW.

So, what do I mean by "setting an intention"? I mean identify what you are hoping to get out of this conversation with another person.

- Are you trying to get insight into their world or their perspective?

- Do you want them to share a behind-the-scenes look at their life or their business?
- Are you trying to get them to share something motivational?

I want you to ask yourself before every guest interaction, "What is the actual purpose of this interview?"

SET A TIME LIMIT FOR THE INTERVIEW

The timeline is so important. Depending on how long your podcast episodes usually are, you'll want to know exactly how long you're going to talk to your guest. Make sure that they know ahead of time how long the podcast interview is going to be. This helps both of you manage your expectations of the call.

For example, my podcast interviews tend to last between thirty and forty-five minutes. I like to let the conversation flow naturally. And a thought I always have in the back of my mind is, "If we go over time, we can always split this episode into two." My other thought is, "My main goal is to pull every ounce of valuable information out of this conversation."

Always set your intention and your time limit.

The Actual Interview Process

Now, here is the piece of the puzzle you've been waiting for: the actual interview process. Yes, I could've given this to you on one page with a quick bulleted task list, but you'd be missing so much. Because a podcast interview isn't something to just check off of your list. Making the scheduling process easy, creating a seamless system, and setting intentions, expectations, and timelines are super important to the overall experience of your podcast guests. Amazing podcast interviews are what will keep listeners coming back to your show years from now. But I do know the logistics are important, so let's dive into those now.

THE ACTUAL INTERVIEW PROCESS:

1. CHECK YOUR EQUIPMENT
    - If you've ever listened to *The Proffitt Podcast*, you may know this story. But for the sake of full-disclosure in this book, I'm going to share my horror story of my very first podcast interview here!

    We'd just moved into our new house a few months before. And being excited about having an actual office, not just a desk setup in the entryway of our house, we decided to purchase a beautiful new desk.

But as it turns out, the desk we ordered from the furniture company was broken. So, when did they decide to deliver the new desk? On the day of my very first podcast interview. When I initially scheduled the furniture delivery, I didn't think anything of it. It was just another day of the week. But when the delivery guys rang our doorbell an hour and a half before my interview, my first thought was, "Oh crap! I literally have to take everything off this desk for them to move the new one in!"

Thankfully, these guys weren't playing around and were ready to move on to the next job! They delivered the new desk, this time with a fully functioning drawer, and were on their way in under an hour.

"Okay, I have plenty of time to set everything back up before my interview," I told myself as I put my computer back on the desk and set the microphone in the same place I'd had it on the other desk. What I failed to realize was that the microphone doesn't actually work unless you plug it back into the computer! (Cue a Homer Simpson "D'oh!" moment!)

I wasn't aware of my mistake until after I'd spoken to my guest for more than forty-five minutes, ended the interview, and went to listen to the audio file. [Insert MANY expletives!] I felt so dumb.

The moral of the story is to always check your equipment.

2. CONNECT TO YOUR INTERVIEW
   RECORDING PLATFORM
   - I wish I could tell you that there is one
     podcast interview platform that is a magical
     unicorn for everyone, but that's just not the
     case. I've had success with a few awesome
     platforms, and I've been sick to my stomach
     over others where I lost two incredible
     interviews! So, they are definitely not all
     created equal. But I will say there are a few
     things to consider when choosing your
     podcast interview platform:
     - Budget (Free vs. Paid)
       - There are great platforms out
         there for free, but they do come
         with limitations that are related
         to the number of guests or time
         allowed. However, I have done
         a good majority of my podcast
         interviews using my free Zoom
         account. As of the publishing of
         this book, you are able to record
         conversations for podcasts
         between two people for free for
         an unlimited amount of time,
         and among three or more for
         up to forty minutes.

- As far as paid programs go, I suggest checking out Buzzsprout's post about remote recording. They definitely do their research when it comes to podcast platforms and they offer a variety of options for paid programs to record your podcast.[1]"How to Record Long Distance Podcast Interviews" - Buzzsprout.com
  - Guest Comfort Level
    - I don't know about you, but I don't want to learn a brand-new software for every podcast interview that I do. That's why I like to use Zoom, because most people in my industry are familiar with it from team meetings and consulting calls.
    - I've also done more technical podcast interviews that require me to record my own audio and the host to record their audio. Then they put the two

---

[1] "How to Record Long-Distance Podcast Interviews"
https://www.buzzsprout.com/blog/long-distance-podcast-recording

tracks into one episode. While this is a great option for two podcasters doing an interview - since they already know how to use audio recording software - it's not great for people who don't understand this type of software. Keep that in mind as you choose a platform for you and your guests.

3. ADJUST VOLUME WHENEVER YOUR GUEST JOINS
   - Make sure both of you can hear each other and neither of your microphones are too loud or too quiet. You want to optimize the sound for the podcast interview, but you also want to make sure your guests can hear you properly.
   - This is also a good opportunity to listen for any distracting noises in the background. Can you hear your kids watching Disney Plus? Do you hear the dog barking from outside the guest's door? Can you hear your neighbors mowing their lawn? Some of these things may be out of your control, but if you can minimize the background noises when

you first jump on an interview, this is the
time to do it.

4. MAKE SURE THEIR EQUIPMENT SOUNDS
   GOOD
   - Similar to making sure their microphone
     sounds great, I suggest each of my guests use
     earbuds or some other type of headphones.
     When they do this, it promotes a better-
     sounding audio track and reduces the risk of
     recording someone's voice twice. When you
     speak, your voice goes into their speakers.
     When they speak, their voice goes into your
     speakers.
   - As the person who is usually recording a
     podcast interview, I've learned the audio
     usually turns out fine as long as I have my
     headphones in. But still, have them use
     earbuds to promote better sound quality if
     possible.

5. CHAT WITH THEM FOR A FEW MINUTES TO
   CALM EVERYONE'S NERVES
   - A casual conversation goes a long way. Take
     a few minutes to go over expectations,
     refresh their memory on what you'd like to
     talk about, and answer any last-minute

questions. The conversations always end up more engaging and relatable when I take a few minutes to really get to know my guests outside of a short, two-to-three sentence bio. Remember, you're trying to be a gracious host!

6. START RECORDING AND LOOK AT THE CLOCK
    - This may sound super simple and glaringly obvious, but this is one of my podcast interview tricks: I always look at the clock when I start recording. I learned early on that I tend to ramble and keep asking questions that I'm genuinely curious about but that may have nothing to do with the podcast episode we're working on. So, to combat my temptation to go down multiple rabbit holes, I look at the clock when I press Record and start an internal timer for when I should be wrapping the interview up. Make sure you know exactly what time you started the interview so you can pace yourself and your questions accordingly.

7. PACE YOURSELF THROUGH QUESTIONS

- Podcast interviews are definitely a skill. You have to find your sweet spot between not taking too long on any one question and not rushing your guests through important details. You'll find your pace the more interviews you do, but just know when you're getting started that the process may feel a little clunky at first. Don't sweat it! You'll be better on your tenth interview than you were on your first!

8. GIVE THEM AN OPPORTUNITY TO PROMOTE
   - Part of being a gracious host is to not make everything about you! You want to give your guests an opportunity to talk about the latest thing they have going on in their business, their products and services, or other promotions they are working on.
   - Have a set time limit, and even tell them ahead of time (in your podcast show guidelines) what they can promote and for how long. You don't want to feel bad having to cut someone off because they talked about an event they have coming up for ten minutes straight. (*Awkward!*) Make your expectations clear before the interview, but

definitely give your guests an opportunity to shine the light on themselves and the cool things they are working on!

9. THANK THEM FOR COMING ON THE SHOW, AND STOP RECORDING
   - This feels like something I shouldn't have to add to this list, but being a Texas girl, I know southern charm goes a long way! So, I always make it a point to thank my guest for coming on the show while we are still recording. I love hearing a host's genuine appreciation of podcast guests when I'm listening to shows. A genuine "Thank you" goes a long way!
   - After you have ended the interview, you want to make sure that you stop recording. You don't want the editing process filled with more audio to cut out at the end. Trust me, it's a lot easier to stop recording and then continue your conversation "off the record" than to find the end of your conversation for the podcast interview and have to go back and cut out all the extra chitchat. (This is a lesson I've learned the hard way!)

After the Interview

10. FOLLOW UP WITH AIR DATES AND OTHER ADDITIONAL INFORMATION

- This is like a bonus step that can help you develop an ongoing relationship with your podcast guest for potential future collaborations and other networking opportunities. Take a few minutes to make sure they have the info they need or follow up with them before their interview airs. Make sure that you have their bio and/or headshot for marketing purposes. Tell them when you expect their interview to air, and ask them to share the episode with their network whenever it comes out.

And that's it! I know we covered a lot in this chapter, but I think going into the detail that we did will set you up for success and better conversations with your podcast guests. I encourage you to check out the resources for podcast interviews on *The Proffitt Podcast* and my YouTube channel to see further tutorials and demonstrations of interviews in action.

I'm not going to pretend that I know all there is to know about hiring someone to create your podcast artwork or music.

However, I've definitely learned a few things over the last few years of running an online business that I hope you consider as you embark on this podcast journey.

Chapter 10: Podcast Artwork & Music

CHAPTER 10: PODCAST ARTWORK & MUSIC

"I'm so confused when it comes to artwork and music for my podcast."

New podcasters often second-guess themselves on whether they chose the right graphic for their podcast artwork or the right music for their show. They want something that will resonate with their audience in a massive way, but the truth is, you won't know until you try something. So, I want you to go into the creative endeavor of picking (or designing) your podcast artwork and developing your show music with an open mind. Remember that you can always change it later if something doesn't work out. Now, let's get started with your podcast artwork.

Podcast Artwork

Up to this point, we have discovered a lot of things on our podcast journey. Hopefully, you understand exactly who you're talking to and the message you want to share, and you've honed in on the type of content you're going to produce. All of your hard work up to this point is really going to pay off in the launch and marketing phases that follow this chapter, and it will also pay off as you choose your podcast artwork.

Here are a few questions I get asked a lot about creating a logo for a podcast:

- What needs to be on it?
- Does it need to have my picture?
- Does it need to have a graphic?
- Do I need to hire a designer?
- Can I create this myself?

There are so many questions and various answers to each of them, but I'm a firm believer in keeping it simple. Let me say that again: "Keep it simple!" Do what feels right to you, right now. It's not like you have to decide on the podcast artwork that will define your mark on the podcasting world forever! I actually love seeing how huge podcasts have rebranded over the years. Here's a perfect example that's relevant as I write this book: the RISE podcast by Rachel Hollis.

If you aren't familiar with Rachel Hollis, I encourage you to check out her work. She is a number one *New York Times Bestselling Author*, motivational speaker, producer of multiple podcasts (she recently even started her own podcast network), and an award winner for her top-rated RISE podcast! But if you've been following her journey for some time, you know she had a completely different podcast when she started. It was called "Dais Podcast." The premise of the show was the same—motivation and inspiration—but the artwork was different from what it is today. So Rachel Hollis is living proof: I want you to keep an open mind as you select your artwork, knowing that, if you decide to change later, it's okay.

I've changed the artwork for my podcast as well. When I first started *The Rookie Life*, which I later rebranded to *The Proffitt Podcast*, I used a picture of me wearing my glasses and holding a cup of coffee on my parent's front porch. Now, my podcast artwork consists of me in front of my microphone smiling and being super intense, as I tend to do during my podcast. And who knows, I may change it again in the next year or two. Don't be afraid to experiment and try new things. Get creative. Come up with a ton of ideas. Treat it like it's all a big experiment, and have fun during this process.

PRO TIP: I encourage you to check out other podcasts' artwork to see how they create theirs. Remember podcast modeling from Chapter 5? You can use that technique to develop your podcast artwork, too.

SHOULD I BE ON MY PODCAST ARTWORK?

The most specific artwork question I get is, "Should I be on the cover?" This really boils down to personal preference. I decided to put my picture on my podcast because it felt right. That's really it. I wish I had some other advice that is scientific proof your podcast does better with or without your headshot. But I don't. I just went with my gut and put my picture on the logo.

Plus, I don't know anyone that specializes in graphics and animations that could have done something within the timeline I had set to rebrand my podcast. I went with what worked. It's what it is for now, and who knows when it'll change again. Don't get me wrong, I like my logo. But I'm not completely married to it.

One final note: while's okay to change things up with your podcast, it is important not to change things *too often* once you settle on one particular logo. Keep the artwork the same for at least six to twelve months so your podcast branding has a chance to work.

SHOULD I PUT MY NAME ON MY PODCAST ARTWORK?

Unless you're a big-name superstar, it's probably not going to matter right now anyway. Ouch. Maybe that's being too brutally honest, but it's the truth. Unless you're someone like Oprah, leave it off. For me, it didn't make sense to call my podcast *The Proffitt Podcast with Krystal Proffitt—Start, Launch, Market*, because that's too long. You may be saying, "Krystal, you just said to not include your name. Do you think of yourself as a celebrity, since you have your name in the title?" Ha! No. Not at all. But, as we discussed in Chapter 2 about picking the title of your podcast, I wanted to use my last name as a play on words. (Come on, it's a podcast for entrepreneurs. I'd be dumb to not include the last name Proffitt.)

SHOULD I DESIGN MY PODCAST ARTWORK OR HIRE A DESIGNER?

Again, this all goes back to your personal preference and budget. What can you afford? If you can barely afford to pay for your podcast hosting services (which we'll get to in Chapter 13), then maybe you should go with the DIY approach to your artwork. I personally love Canva. As of publishing this book, their services are free, and they have incredible graphic design tools. There are paid options and upgrades for images and graphics, but I've been using the free version of Canva since 2014. So just know that anything is possible when you get a little scrappy. This is the perfect option if you can't afford a graphic designer.

But maybe you're saying, "Yeah, it looks easy, but I'm not artistic. I don't think I'll be able to make something that's really *wow!*" Well, you know yourself better than anyone else. Consider hiring a graphic designer. And if you don't know personally know any graphic designers, don't sweat it. I have some resources I would love for you to check out.

- UpWork.com
- Fiverr.com
- FreeeUp.com
- 99Designs.com

I'm sure there are a million other sites out there like these, but these are the ones I've either used or been referred to by people I trust. On these freelance sites, you can find tons of talented graphic designers with lots of experience. But always make sure you're finding someone who is highly rated and fits within your price range.

CHOOSING A FREELANCER

You may have a budget that allows you to pay someone thousands of dollars for a podcast logo, or you may only have a budget of twenty dollars. Obviously, the quality between the two price points is going to vary, and it may take several inquiries with different freelancers to find someone to collaborate with. But if trying to figure out how to create your podcast artwork is something that's going to hold you back from launching, then hire it out. Have someone else do it, and take that burden off of yourself so you can focus your attention on your podcast launch.

Podcast Music

Let's think back to all of the podcast modeling you did in Chapter 5: the shows you love, the ones you couldn't stand, the ones that make the biggest impact on you, and the ones you want to emulate. (Notice I didn't say "copy." We aren't trying to make cookie cutter podcasts 'round here!) Was there any background music that stood out to you? What about the way it flowed? Did it flow perfectly from the intro to the episode and then the outro like butter on a nice, warm biscuit in smooth, perfect podcast harmony? (Okay, weird segue there, but anyway.) I want you to pay attention to what you love about those episodes and what you don't, because it matters.

FINDING YOUR PODCAST MUSIC

Music isn't a requirement. There are tons of podcasts that don't have any music in them at all. Not in the intro. Not between ads. Not in the outro. Nowhere. So, don't feel like you have to have music in your podcast if you're just not "feeling it." However, if you are, there are two options for you to consider:

- Find royalty-free music online
- Hire a music producer

ONLINE ROYALTY-FREE MUSIC

I've got to be totally honest: I'm not a huge fan of grabbing royalty-free music online. I'm sure it has to do with my risk-averse nature to be overly cautious about copyrights and not infringing on someone's creativity in any way. (A paralegal friend told me one time, "The worst they can do is send you a cease-and-desist letter." Even still, my stomach turned. No thanks! I'm good!) However, I do know there are reputable sites out there. My only word of caution to you is to make sure you read the fine print on every transaction you make online. Or anywhere. Period.

HIRE A MUSIC PRODUCER

What do you do in order to hire someone to produce custom music for you? What does the process actually look like? I have a few tips and strategies you can use as well as some personal examples of how this has worked for me.

CHECK THEIR RATINGS AND REVIEWS

The freelance websites I've mentioned before (Upwork, Fiverr, Freeeup) usually have a rating or ranking system that shows you the individual's expertise, level of accomplishment, or prior work. They should have some sort of star rating - for example, an average of 4.5 stars for thirty clients.

My husband and I are big on reviews. We won't try a new restaurant, make a big purchase, or sometimes even rent a movie online unless we've thoroughly researched the ratings and reviews. It's just as important to look at these when you're choosing people to work with. (I wish we had known the ratings and reviews of the hotel we stayed in once that had red Kool Aid stains on the carpet and smelled like moth balls. Turns out, it had a 1.5-star rating. I didn't sleep at all that night because I thought a cockroach was going to crawl in bed and snuggle with me. Ew, it still gives me chills.) Ratings and reviews matter!

STICK TO YOUR BUDGET

Please don't break the bank for your podcast music. I'll be totally upfront with you, I only spent thirty dollars on my podcast music. I know, that kind of feels like I'm cheating or something, but I didn't spend a ton of money. I don't think that you have to. Set a number that you're comfortable with before you start the inquiry process.

MUSIC LICENSING

There was a cool experience I had last year as I learned how licensing music rights work. I've followed this musician and his wife on Instagram for a while and admire both. And while I think that could be a possible route I eventually want to go, I haven't been able to invest that kind of money in my podcast music, yet. But here's how that interaction went down:

[Sent Via Instagram Direct Message]
"Hi, _____!
Big fan of yours…
Love following your journey…
I had a music question for you. Would you be interested in producing a short instrumental track for a podcast?
I'm rebranding and looking for some original music. I enjoy your vibe and talent. Just thought I would reach out. Look forward to hearing from you.
-Krystal"

[His Response]
"Hey Krystal! Thanks so much for thinking of me for this. I am very grateful. What's the best e-mail for you? I'll shoot over some questions and then we can decide any next steps from there. Thanks again."

From there, we discussed what I was looking for and the overall vibe of the music I wanted, and he sent me to some more samples of his work. Although we didn't end up collaborating, I learned so much in the process. Don't be afraid to get creative and reach out to people you know in the music community. You might be surprised who says yes to creating custom music for your podcast.

WHAT DO YOU ASK THEM FOR?

As with everything else we've discussed, music needs vary from podcast to podcast. But if you're just looking for a baseline of what to ask for in music production, I suggest you start here.

1. Tell the musician you're looking for a thirty to sixty-second track of instrumental music to play in the background. This could be the background music for your main podcast theme or for your self-sponsored ads, but I suggest having one main track between thirty and sixty seconds long.
2. The next thing to do is tell them you want a five to fifteen-second sweeper. This is the music you hear at the very end of *The Proffitt Podcast*. It's a fifteen-second standalone audio clip that sounds very similar to the track that's in my main

podcast theme. This track helps the listener know that you're wrapping things up. I've also listened to other podcasts where they use these short clips strategically in their ads or within their show to transition between segments. For example, the intro to an ad segment, back to the interview segment, and then back to the outro. This track helps everything flow well. But I do suggest having those in two separate tracks as opposed to trimming five seconds out of the main theme music.

Tips for Hiring Someone

I'm not going to pretend that I know all there is to know about hiring someone to create your podcast artwork or music. However, I've definitely learned a few things over the last few years of running an online business that I hope you consider as you embark on this podcast journey.

ALWAYS ASK FOR REFERENCES

We touched on this earlier when we talked about reviews and ratings, but let's talk about references and prior work. You definitely want to know that the person you're paying to produce your music has done this before. You don't want to waste anyone's time dealing with an individual who doesn't have it together. You want to know what kind of work they do and have done in the past. If you're looking for something that's upbeat and spunky to boost your audience's energy, you *don't* want someone who produces calm, classical music for studying. (I think about the music playing on the Titanic as the ship is sinking. You hear it now, too, don't you? A little Celine Dion "My Heart Will Go On" played in your head, right?) While that music definitely has its time and place, it doesn't match the vibe I want for my podcast. And the vibe I want may not match the vibe you want! So, make sure you find someone with a similar vibe to yours.

ALWAYS PROVIDE SONG REFERENCES

When you're about to listen to someone's previous work, have two to three songs in mind as a reference point. For example, let's say you love pop music, and you want something that's high energy. Give your potential producer two or three songs as the benchmark. This helps you and your potential hires know what you're looking for and when you've found it. Never go into a potential collaboration and say, "I don't really know what I want...just have fun with it." They could come back with something that's an absolute terrible fit for you and your audience! This doesn't mean it's bad music; it simply means it's bad for your podcast. Give your music producer all the tools they need to succeed. This will minimize the back and forth and shorten the timeline to produce your music. You could also consider sending them podcast episodes you enjoy.

KNOW YOUR BUDGET

We've already talked about staying within your budget, but let's dive a little deeper into actual price. I really want this to hit home. Make sure you are crystal clear on pricing. Again, we're trying to minimize the back-and-forth messaging, but we also want to set expectations for who to work with. You don't want to get too far down the road with someone before you discover that they're going to charge $750 when you can only pay $20. That doesn't sound like a fun conversation for anybody to have. From the very first interaction, be clear on your budget with a music producer.

READ THE FINE PRINT

[Disclaimer: I have no qualifications to give legal advice. Zero. Everything expressed here is simply my own opinion.]
Speaking of risk-averse behavior, I'm a stickler for reading the fine print on any and all transactions I make online. There are website policies, contracts, fine print, and terms of use for anything anybody creates

for you. Make sure that you read these policies carefully. Maybe you're saying, "Krystal, come on. I know this stuff already. I'm careful." You probably are. But did you know there are many websites out there that offer "royalty-free music" and then state in their fine print that it's "not for use on podcasts"? (Ruh-roh, Shaggy!)

WHAT TO LOOK FOR IN THE FINE PRINT

Be clear on how revisions work if you're not happy with a producer's first efforts. Do they offer money-back guarantees if you're not satisfied with the finished product? Are there any kind of cancellation policies? Always pay attention to the fine print when you're working with someone else.

Well, we did it. You now have all the knowledge you need to start a podcast. Hooray! But, hold up: the real work is about to begin. I know, you've already learned so much and I've asked a lot of you: from choosing your equipment and picking a podcast name to finding your audience and getting comfortable with your content. We've talked about choosing software, recording some episodes, and even being brave enough to step out of your comfort zone and interview someone else. And I just want to take a second to say that **I am so proud of you.**

If you take everything you've learned up to this point and put it into action, the next phases will be a piece of cake! I know it's been hard work, but keep going. Because believe it or not, you've already been through the hardest part of this podcasting journey. The rest of it is getting your show launched and marketing the crap out of it. Now, let's go launch your podcast out into the world.

Krystal Proffitt

Many new podcasters think, "It's easy. I just hit publish, and my podcast is out into the world. Why do anything else?"

Please don't do that.

Chapter 11: Announce Your Podcast Launch Date

CHAPTER 11: ANNOUNCE YOUR PODCAST LAUNCH DATE

"How can I get the most momentum out of launching my podcast?"

This is one of the easiest questions I get to answer, but my response is often what brand-new podcasters don't want to hear: Announce your podcast launch date as soon as you know it. The immediate responses I get back are, "But that's six months from now!" and "What if I'm not ready when the date actually comes?" and "What if I need to postpone? I don't have all the details figured out yet." All these responses are based out of fear.

Fear that you won't be done in time.
Fear of not being ready to launch.
Fear of actually putting your content out into the world.
Fear that you're not good enough.

I get it. I've had all of these fears and worries too. But if you don't have a specific goal to aim for - your podcast launch date - then how are you ever going to hit it?

Instead of lecturing you on intangible ways to overcome fear, I wanted to give you some practical tools that can help you announce your podcast launch date so you gain as much momentum as possible from day one.

The Podcast Launch Runway

"What are some things I can do so my audience is ready to listen when my podcast goes live?"

That's where the podcast launch runway comes into play, which is a baby step into your actual podcast launch. There's a YouTube video I watched last year with Christy Wright, who's the Ramsey Personality behind the Business Boutique organization, and Stu McLaren, an expert in membership sites and the founder of Tribe. In this video, they talked about the importance of launching, well, anything.[2] And because I know these two are rock stars in the online marketing world, I was hooked on their every word. While they were chatting, Christy asked Stu about the importance of a launch runway.

I've been involved with several big book launches over the years, and a few by number-one *New York Times* best-selling authors. I saw firsthand the behind-the-scenes details that go into pulling off big book launches: the audience surveys, the details of the target audience, implementing as much word-of-mouth marketing as possible. It's the stuff I totally geek out

---

[2] ("Pulling Off a Great Launch with Stu McLaren," https://www.youtube.com/watch?v=QbaUg1vaEo8)

on! So, I thought I knew all there was to know about launching something with success. Turns out, my knowledge was barely scratching the surface.

In their video, Stu said something that literally blew my mind that I'd never thought about before. He said something to the effect of, "How do you think a movie becomes a blockbuster? Because the previews start coming out six months to a year before the movie is in theaters!" Anytime a *Star Wars* movie or any other Disney movie comes out, you know about it. Why? Because they start promoting them early!

I remember munching on buttery popcorn and chocolate almonds with my boys in the theater when a preview for *Toy Story 4* lit up the screen. The four of us glanced back and forth at each other as the characters came to life on the screen. Then the trailer ended with the air date. "Oh man, it doesn't come out until *next summer*," I told the boys with disappointment. "I guess we'll have to wait until then." That's how far in advance they planted the seed. They knew exactly what they were doing. As it got closer to opening weekend, we started to see Buzz Lightyear and Woody show up in fast food chains and movie ads everywhere. They were telling us, "Watch. This movie is going to be a blockbuster." It had a huge launch runway to build up anticipation and provide sneak peeks of what was to come. Pixar did a great job of building excitement.

Seeing the characters our family has grown to love over the years come back to the screen filled all of us with joy and enthusiasm. (And yes, we did go see the movie in the theaters during its opening week.) Think of ways to create your own blockbuster for your podcast launch.

Intro to the Podcast Launch

"I'm not ready to launch my podcast today. Why would I tell people I am?"

If you haven't already, I want to encourage you to listen to Episode 48 of The Proffitt Podcast: "How to Launch a Podcast."[3] The podcast launch is an essential piece of the puzzle that not a lot of people pay attention to. And it shows. That's why a lot of podcasts don't have the traction that they want from day one.

HOW TO PICK YOUR PODCAST LAUNCH DATE

Launching a podcast is the most overlooked part of the entire podcast process. Many new podcasters think, "It's easy. I just hit publish, and my podcast is out into the world. Why do anything else?" Please don't do that.

There is a strategy behind picking the right podcast launch date for you. Let's talk about the things you need to consider, what questions to ask yourself, and

---

[3] "Ep 48: How to Launch a Podcast, The Proffitt Podcast" (https://krystalproffitt.com/episode48)

how to find the right time in your calendar. So, let's find out when you should launch your podcast!

1. LOOK AT YOUR PERSONAL CALENDAR

What's going on in your life right now? What season of life are you in? Do you have small kids at home so you have to escape to your closet to record your podcast? Are you working around multiple calendars, including school projects, work deadlines, family obligations, and kids' activities? Do you have a big event coming up, like a wedding or graduation? Are the holidays right around the corner?

If you're looking to launch your podcast soon, take a look at the next few months. What's realistic? What's really going to work for you? I'm not going to lie - I *want* you to launch your podcast as quick as humanly possible! You can only know what content works and what doesn't when you actually start putting content out into the world.

But I also know that if you rush the podcast launch process and do it at a time when it doesn't work for you personally, two things will happen:

- You're going to burn out shortly after you start.
- You won't be able to stay consistent with your podcast because you didn't plan accordingly.

Make sure you take a good look at your personal calendar and use that as a reference when picking your podcast launch date.

2. LOOK AT YOUR PROFESSIONAL CALENDAR

When can your business benefit the most from you launching your podcast? When can you actually dedicate time for the launch?

Maybe you already have your own business. Or maybe you have a full-time job while you're trying to start a podcast. Look at your professional calendar and see when a good time for your podcast launch will be. Is it six months from now after work slows down a little bit? Is it over a holiday period because you know you'll be able to pay more attention to the launch strategy? Launching requires more attention than just day-to-day, week-to-week content creation. You have to develop a plan, outline your strategy, and execute it with your podcast launch goals in mind.

3. LOOK AT YOUR PROMOTIONAL CALENDAR

What's coming up in the next few weeks within your industry?

If you're in the health and fitness industry, maybe the best time for you to launch your podcast is in January, when people are setting new personal goals for themselves and looking for motivation. Or maybe take a look at when other podcasters in your industry launched and see their results. Did someone else have huge success launching in the summer? Did they do a huge ramp-up leading up to their launch? I don't think we should ever compare ourselves to others, but I also am a strong believer in podcast modeling. It's why I teach it to my clients and students in Proffitt Podcasting, and it can make all the difference when you're trying to make the big decisions for your podcast. You don't need to copy someone or compare your podcast to theirs. Just trying to understand why they did something and how they did it can be a very powerful tool.

4. WHEN WILL YOU HAVE ENOUGH CONTENT READY TO LAUNCH?

Are you currently still struggling to create content ideas? Are you still trying to figure out how to record and set up your equipment? Or are you cranking out episodes and screaming, "Bring it on!!"

In Episode 48, "How to Launch a Podcast," I tell you all about the podcast launch plan, which we will go into massive detail about in Chapter 14. In the launch plan, we go into the exact steps and make a checklist for what needs to happen before you launch. One of the important checklist items is having at least three to five episodes for people to listen to when your podcast launches. So, as you think about picking your podcast launch date, I want you to give yourself a reality check.

If you want to realistically launch your podcast in the next three months, for example, what would it take to create enough content to make that happen? I want you to be really honest with yourself.

At the end of the day if your expectations aren't realistic, you're going to let yourself down more than anyone else. Do a gut check right now on everything we just went over. Then, go with a podcast launch date that fits into all aspects of your schedule. The important thing is to pick a date and stick with it!

How to Announce Your Podcast Launch Date

Okay, we're here. It's go time! You have to *actually* announce your podcast launch date. I know that from the very beginning you've been telling people what you're up to. You've told your family and friends and strangers online, "I'm going to create a podcast!" Maybe you've been gathering data on your future audience. Maybe you've polled your ideal listener. "What do you want to hear? What topics do you want me to talk about?"

It's finally time to put that stake in the ground and announce your podcast launch date. There are several ways you can do this, and you may find even more inspiration when we talk about launching your podcast in Chapter 14, but here are some ideas to get you started:

- Graphics on social media
  - Make a Facebook or Instagram post with the podcast logo and launch date
    - You can also upload to Facebook and Instagram Stories
  - Upload a Facebook or Instagram Stories video announcing the date
- Tweet something like, "My new podcast will be here on [Insert Date]!"
- Pin an image to Pinterest
- Share a sound bite on LinkedIn
- Put your logo and launch date in the banner of a Facebook page or group
- Add graphics to your website ("Coming Soon" images are fun!)
- Send an e-mail to your audience with the launch date

I know exactly what you're thinking right now: "Krystal, I'm not ready. I'm not going to be ready. You're telling me to announce my podcast, but I don't even know how to do everything yet!" It's okay. I hear the frustration in your voice, and I understand your hesitation. But I also want you to remember that you've committed to launching your podcast. You want to do this. You have your why. You know exactly why you're doing this, right? So, you're going to pick a date, and you're going to commit to it.

And you're going to remember that it doesn't have to be perfect. You don't have to have everything figured out and in the right place for this to work. You just have to get going. And you're going to make mistakes. I've made plenty of (dumb) mistakes, but I've kept going. I attribute a lot of my consistency in my personal life and my business to the ability to pick what I'm focused on - whether it's a date, a deadline or a goal - and stick to it.

I'm challenging you to pick a podcast launch date and

stick with it. Announce to the world that something

incredible is coming. Something you've worked hard

on is about to be released out into the wild. And I

promise, before you know it, you'll have your very own

podcast!

Krystal Proffitt

There's no doubt about it, podcast descriptions can be confusing. So, let's break down the difference between a podcast description versus an episode description.

Chapter 12: Podcast Descriptions & Show Notes

CHAPTER 12: PODCAST DESCRIPTIONS AND SHOW NOTES

"What the heck are podcast descriptions and show notes?"

There's a lot of confusion around what constitutes show notes and where they live. And another thing many podcasters get confused about is the difference between a podcast description and an episode description. Why are these important? Why do they matter? And how can we use them with your podcast? Well, let's dive in!

SEO FOR YOUR PODCAST

Both your descriptions and show notes are very important for SEO purposes. What is SEO? That stands for "search engine optimization," and we'd be here for hours if we dug into all the nuances of SEO. So, for the sake of time, I want you to know that the more keywords you have associated with your podcast, the more likely that you are going to show up in search results, whether that's in search engines like Google or podcast directories like Apple Podcasts, Spotify, Google Play, etc. - basically, all the places you're going to connect your podcast. This is why descriptions and show notes are really important, especially because

Google now indexes podcasts in search results alongside blog posts and YouTube videos.

Let's go back to the keywords you chose for your podcast in Chapter 4. You want to make sure to sprinkle those specific phrases throughout your descriptions and show notes for your podcast. But there is a balance! You don't want to overstuff keywords into your podcast descriptions and show notes because you think it will help them get found it easier. Technology on the internet is smarter than that, and you'll get red-flagged very quickly! (Keyword stuffing is a big no-no!)

Podcast Description

"Which one goes to your hosting site, and which one do you use for each individual episode?"

There's no doubt about it, podcast descriptions can be confusing. So, let's break down the difference between a podcast description versus an episode description. A *podcast* description is the information you add to your hosting site when you first set up your podcast. This is what shows up on all of the platforms where listeners find podcasts.

If you were to look up *The Proffitt Podcast* right now on Apple Podcasts or Spotify or any other podcast platform, you'd see my podcast description. But I'll do you one better - I'll give it to you:

"The Proffitt Podcast" Podcast Description

Hi, I'm Krystal, your host of The Proffitt Podcast. Have you ever found yourself asking, "What equipment do I need to start a podcast? What is the best way to launch? How can I get more downloads? What does it take to market a podcast?" Then you're in the right place, my friend.

Entrepreneurs dream of creating deeper connections with their audience, but they're totally overwhelmed with the thought of podcasting. On this podcast, I strip down the process and take all of the overwhelm away.

With my three-step approach (Start, Launch, and Market), I deliver content to help you take action and create a podcast your audience craves. I've worked with online business owners wanting to have a better marketing strategy, just like you, and individuals who aren't even sure what a podcast is.

The motto around here is, "We all have to start somewhere."

Join us every Tuesday and Thursday for new episodes on how you can Start, Launch, and Market your own podcast.

WHAT TO INCLUDE IN YOUR PODCAST DESCRIPTION:

There are four main points to consider as your compile your podcast description:

- **WHAT** is your podcast about?
- **WHO** is your podcast for?
- **WHEN** do you publish new episodes?
- **WHAT** value do you offer?

If we go back and break down my podcast description, then it would look like this:

- **WHAT** your podcast is about: *How to start, launch, and market your podcast*
- **WHO** your podcast is for: *Entrepreneurs*
- **WHEN** you publish new episodes: *Every Tuesday & Thursday*
- **WHAT** value you offer: *I'm offering entrepreneurs value by answering their questions about how to start, launch, and market a podcast*

Now that you know what goes into a podcast description, use podcast modeling again to go check out some of your favorite podcasts. What do their descriptions say? Do they include how often they're going to publish new episodes? Do they call out who their audience is? Do they tell you what they're going to talk about?

Episode Descriptions

"Are episode descriptions show notes?"

Some people refer to them as show notes, but not me. For the sake of this book, and any other way we could possibly cross paths, I want to make it very clear that your episode descriptions are *not* show notes. These are describing the content that's in your episode, but they don't give as much detail as the show notes do. In a nutshell, the episode descriptions are the high-level summary of what's going on in your podcast, but not everything that's happening!

How long can these episode descriptions be? I know that Apple Podcasts only allows for 4,000 characters. Though, I've never found myself getting too close to the limit. And again, keywords are so important when you're writing up these episode descriptions for your podcast, especially since Google has started indexing podcast episodes! (That's amazing news for all of us podcasters!) Make sure to do your keyword research for your episode descriptions.

I was resistant to keyword research for a long time. I kept saying, "I don't have time for that! Does it really work?" I'm telling you, make time. It works!

DO PEOPLE REALLY READ THOSE?

Don't simply string together a few words to create your episode descriptions. "It's fine. No one really reads these anyway." Nope. That's not the mentality we're going to have. I want you to put a lot of thought into the copy that you use to describe your episodes. I'll be honest, I don't read other podcasts' episode descriptions either. But that's not why they're important!

There's a specific reason we're doing it this way. In Chapter 15, I'll show you how to use this same exact information in your marketing strategy. So, it's really important that you don't just throw something out there with zero effort.

Do the work. Do it right from the beginning.

Because life gets so much easier when you're not starting from scratch. You'll be able to repurpose the episode descriptions that you've already taken time to write really well.

WHEN DO YOU CREATE EPISODE DESCRIPTIONS?

I write my episode descriptions after I've created the episode and uploaded it to my hosting site, which we're getting to in the next chapter. This step is actually one of the very last things I do before I publish an episode. And there are two very specific reasons:

1. I know what the podcast episode content is about.
2. I know how I want to explain it to my audience.

Podcast Show Notes

Show notes are the Mack-daddy of podcast descriptions. But I want to make something very clear:

SHOW NOTES ARE *NOT* JUST A TRANSCRIPTION OF YOUR PODCAST EPISODES!

No. No. No. Please don't do this!

Your podcast show notes should be a place where listeners can go to get more detailed info about what you're sharing, visit your website and interact with you, or grab any free and even paid resources you're offering. What I love about show notes is how fancy or simple they can be and how easy they are to create!

Now, I know what you're thinking. "Krystal, you say they're easy to create, but they look like a ton of work!" I get it. I felt the exact same way. And I honestly thought about not having show notes at all. But I'm so glad I decided to use them, and I've got a great show notes hack for you today! If you create amazing outlines for your episodes while you're planning and recording, you can turn those into your show notes! **BOOM**...you're welcome! If you put in the time upfront to create an awesome podcast outline, show notes are a piece of cake! Simply format your thoughts in a notebook or a Google Doc and then repurpose that content outline for your website.

Not only is this good for SEO and Google indexing (use those keywords!), but it's also a great way for your listeners to take that next step with your podcast. Maybe you offer more resources on your website. Maybe you can schedule consulting calls with your audience. Maybe you can send them to additional sources of value that'll make them know, like, and trust you even more.

ARE SHOW NOTES BLOG POSTS?

If you're familiar with blog posts, then you'll agree that show notes are very similar, if not identical, to traditional blog posts. The only difference may be that there's an audio file of your podcast episode somewhere on the webpage. Transform your episode outline into show notes that include pictures, video, or something else that adds value. This is also an amazing opportunity to get more traffic to your website, and it gives you more chances to engage with your audience.

Once again, I'm going to encourage you to look at other podcasters who have amazing show notes. (Amy Porterfield from the *Online Marketing Made Easy* podcast is the first podcaster that comes to mind. Go check out her podcast show notes. They are incredibly helpful!)

What If I Don't Have a Website?

This is a valid question and concern for podcasters on a strict budget. But I'm going to tell you what I'd tell a coaching client or student: you *should* have a website. If not, you're missing out on so many opportunities to further your relationship with your audience. Even if it's a basic site without all the bells and whistles, I encourage you to consider a website for your podcast. Some podcast hosts, like Buzzsprout, offer their users a basic website with paid plans. This is a great place to start and can at least get you moving in the right direction.

Now, let's talk about how to actually get your podcast out into the world with your podcast hosting site.

You could have a great plan in place to launch your podcast on a certain date, but if your listeners can't find you on the date because your podcast isn't listed, you're losing out on potential downloads and new listeners from the beginning.

And we don't want that!

Chapter 13: Podcast Hosting Site

CHAPTER 13: PODCAST HOSTING SITE

"What is a podcast hosting site? And how do I find the right one for me?"

You've heard me talk about it a few times, but now I really want to dive into what a podcast hosting site is. If you haven't Googled it by now or heard me talk about it somewhere else, then this is a great time for me to explain it to you. Your hosting site is where your podcast lives online. If you've been wondering, "How in the world do I get connected to all of these different platforms? It seems like so much work to add it Apple Podcasts then Spotify then iHeartRadio then Google Play and Stitcher...each week I have to upload my episode to all these places?" No, you don't have to do that. (Whew! I know, a big sigh of relief, right?)

What Does a Podcast Hosting Site Do?

How does it work then? I want to show you what a hosting site is, how to set up your hosting site, how to upload a trailer episode to get connected to all the platforms, and how to connect to all the directories. If you listen to a podcast in an app (like Apple Podcasts, Google Podcasts, Spotify), then that's where the podcast host plays a role. They do a lot for your podcast, including the following:

- Manage Stats
- Host Podcast Episodes
- Connect Podcast to All of the Platforms
- Manage Audio Files
- Manage RSS Feed
- Categorize Your Podcast

My Preferred Hosting Site

Personally, I use Buzzsprout. I've used them since day one. And while I know there are other podcast hosting sites out there, I don't like to recommend services or products I've never used. So, I'm recommending Buzzsprout.com for your podcast hosting services. They've been an amazing resource for me to turn to when it comes to the technical side of podcasting. They are like the podcast gurus I never knew I needed in my life! And, as of the publication of this book, they offer a free trial for new users. You can test drive their platform before you make a decision.

If you want to learn more about Buzzsprout and see if it's the right fit for you, listen to Episode 73, "Best

Podcasting Hosting Site, Buzzsprout.com," where I interviewed their Head of Content, Travis Albritton.[4]

How to Set Up Your Hosting Site

Note: The information below contains instructions on setting up a podcast through the Buzzsprout platform. The order and appearance of the process may be different for other hosting sites.

Now, let's walk through the steps of setting up your podcast hosting site. We're going to pretend you're a brand-new podcaster who hasn't set anything up and wants to create a free account. (You can definitely go ahead and set up your paid account if you know Buzzsprout is the route you want to go, but I want to keep this simple for anyone, whether you choose a free or paid plan.) Now, let's create your podcast!

1. Create and verify your new podcast account. Select that you're a brand-new podcaster.
2. Go to "Podcast Settings."
3. Enter your podcast info.
   - This is where you'll enter your podcast title and description, upload your podcast artwork, choose your podcast categories, and so forth.

---

[4]Ep 73, "Best Podcast Hosting Site, BuzzSprout" The Proffitt Podcast, https://krystalproffitt.com/episode73/

4. Upload your first (or trailer) episode.
   - I highly recommend putting out a trailer episode first and not your first actual episode. You have to have at least one audio file in order to get connected to all of the podcast directories.
5. Enter the Episode Title.
   - You *do not* have to include numbers in the episode titles. Most platforms default to the number you assign to the episode.
6. Enter the Episode Description.
   - Remember everything we just covered in the last chapter? Time to put that into practice! You can italicize or bold words within your descriptions to make them stand out. You can also include links that go to your website or other URLs.
7. Enter the Episode Summary.
   - Input a few words as to what the episode is about. Sometimes I use my SEO keywords here or re-enter the title of the episode.
8. Input Artist/Guest Information.
   - If you're uploading a solo podcast episode, then your name (as the podcast host) will appear here.

- If you're uploading an interview episode, you would provide the guest's name in this box.
9. Check that your podcast artwork is uploaded.
    - Make sure you uploaded your podcast artwork in podcast settings.
    - I recommend *not* changing your podcast artwork from episode to episode, even if you have a guest on. Leave that to the marketing graphics you'll post on social media or other platforms, but leave the artwork the same in your hosting site for each episode to properly brand your podcast.
10. Input the tags for your episode.
    - These are to further categorize your episodes. I use the keywords I developed for my podcast in the beginning for each episode.
11. Input episode numbers.
    - Enter the season number.
        - I do not have seasons for my podcast. They are all "Season 1." But if you will have seasons, this is where you input that information.
    - Enter the episode number.
        - This is where you'll input whether this is "Episode 0" (which it would be for a trailer episode) or "Episode 1."

- Select the episode type.
    - This is where you select whether this is your trailer, a full episode, or a bonus episode.
12. Select "explicit content" if that's relevant.
    - I personally don't choose to mark any content explicit unless it includes a harsh four-letter word. There are other implications that go into choosing whether content is explicit, but at the end of the day, it's totally subjective. The golden rule for me is, "If my grandmother would be offended listening to this, it should be marked as explicit."
13. Select save and update episode.
    - BOOM! You've just uploaded your first episode!
14. Either publish or schedule the episode.
    - If the audio file you uploaded is your trailer or first episode and you already know your launch date, then feel free to publish this as soon as you feel comfortable.
    - If you're uploading other episodes to be aired in the future, then schedule those for the proper air dates.
    - PRO TIP: I schedule my episodes to air at midnight (12:00 a.m.) for my time zone on the date they are supposed to go live. This

ensures that listeners in other countries don't have to wait longer to listen to my content.

CAN I UPDATE MY PODCAST INFO AFTER I LAUNCH?

Yes, you can absolutely make changes to your podcast information at any time, though the changes may take several hours to show up on all of the platforms where your podcast is listed. I've made lots of changes to my podcast over its lifetime, from rebranding and uploading new artwork to changing the podcast description when I thought of a better way to describe my listeners. So just know that what you input today doesn't have to be the final draft of your podcast. But you have to start somewhere.

Lessons Learned and Things You Need to Know

"If you could go back to the time you were uploading your first episode, what would you tell yourself?"

Such a great question. Because honestly, I didn't know all of this stuff. I made lots of mistakes in the beginning and made the process a lot longer than it has to be. I don't want that for you. So, here are a few tips and things to watch out for as you start uploading your episodes to your podcast hosting site.

- Podcast hosts *don't* accept raw files.
    - Your Audacity file (with the ".aup" ending) cannot be uploaded into your hosting site. The file has to be in an audio format - like MP3 or WAV - in order for your podcast host to accept it.
- It's a lot easier to *schedule podcast episodes* in advance than it is to upload them the day they are supposed to air.
    - The podcast directories update every few hours, so your podcast will not automatically (or magically) appear on all the platforms as soon as you hit publish. Sometimes it takes a while. This is why I recommend airing your episode at midnight the day your episode is set to go live so you can ensure listeners receive their "New Podcast Episode" notifications on their listening devices at the same time each week.

Connecting to Podcast Directories

"But how do I get my podcast to show up on Apple Podcasts, Spotify, Google Play, etc.? Doesn't my hosting site do that?"

Yup! And we're finally on the home stretch of having your podcast completely set up on your hosting site! So, let's get your podcast connected to all the places. The "Directories" section in Buzzsprout is where you'll connect to your podcast to podcast directories.

Let's say you want to start by listing your podcast in Apple Podcasts. Buzzsprout provides step-by-step instructions once you click on each individual podcast directory. But for the sake of teaching, let's go through one of them really quick.

- Click on Apple Podcasts in the "Directories" section of your Buzzsprout account.
- You'll be asked to verify that your info is set up correctly in Podcast Settings.
- Then you'll follow the instructions to submit your RSS feed to Apple Podcasts.
- Check back in on your Buzzsprout account to see when your podcast is listed.
  - You should receive a notification from Apple when your podcast has been accepted.

HOW LONG DOES IT TAKE TO BE ACCEPTED?

As of the printing of this book, it can take from seven to fourteen days for your podcast to be properly uploaded on certain platforms. That's why it's so important to set up your hosting site *before* you start developing your launch plan. You could have a great plan in place to launch your podcast on a certain date, but if your listeners can't find you on the date because your podcast isn't listed, you're losing out on potential downloads and new listeners from the beginning. And we don't want that!

Additional Buzzsprout Resources

I know this chapter is super Buzzsprout focused, but it's because they have been so helpful in my podcast journey, and they want to see their podcast members succeed! (Shout out Buzzsprout! Y'all are awesome!) One of the ways they focus on success for their members is by offering incredible resources. Let's talk about a few of them.

RESOURCES WITHIN YOUR ACCOUNT

There is a dedicated "Resources" tab within your Buzzsprout account that has everything from tutorial videos and helpful blog posts to discounts with partnering companies and available affiliate promotions for Buzzsprout members.

BUZZSPROUT ONLINE COMMUNITY

When I first joined the Buzzsprout Facebook group, there were around a thousand people there. Today, it's exploded into this wonderful community where podcasters (new and seasoned) join together for conversations about equipment, technology, recording, interviewing, best practices, and encouragement. When I feel stuck (and yes, I do still get stuck in my podcast journey!), that's where I turn. I know that the podcasters in that community value different opinions and perspectives, but most importantly it's where I send anyone who asks me a question that I don't know the answer to. (Believe me, there are many equipment and recording scenarios where I'm not the expert!)

PODCAST PLAYERS FOR YOUR WEBSITE

"How do you get your podcast uploaded to your website?" Great question and one that I had in the very beginning as well. I came from a blogging background. I already knew the basics of having a website. So, when I found out that you can embed either single or multi-episode players directly onto your website, I was really excited! This is where my blogging experience interweaved with my podcast to create some awesome show notes. There are plugin players for website builders, but I like to embed them myself. I'm a little bit of a show notes control freak!

STATISTICS

"Where do you find the statistics for your podcast?" There is a dedicated section within Buzzsprout for your stats. From how many downloads per episode your podcast is getting to where listeners are in the world, podcast statistics are where I can really nerd out on you! (Don't worry, I won't. At least, not right now…)

Note: As of the printing of this book, your podcast statistics won't start populating in your Buzzsprout account until you've published at least three episodes. However, if you launch your podcast with three episodes, problem solved!

WEBSITE PROVIDED BY BUZZSPROUT

"Do I need a website for my podcast?" In my opinion, every podcast should have a website! For multiple reasons! But if that's not in your budget right now, that's okay. If you have zero desire to build a website, then Buzzsprout's got you covered. They offer you the ability to create a simple website using their platform. No fancy coding. No complicated backend logistics. Just a full-blown website for you to send listeners to!

For those of you with a website and a little technical know-how, you could redirect a page on your site to your Buzzsprout website. That would give you the ability to have your podcast on your website without having to upload individual episodes and show notes.

Okay, Now What?

Basically, you're ready to rock-n-roll with your podcast. In theory, you have everything you need to know in order to have a full, published podcast. However, we're not stopping here. There are a few more steps to do before you actually launch your podcast. But I want you to take a second and realize how far you've come! You're so close to having a podcast out in the world. I hope you're as excited as I am for you! Now, let's talk about actually launching this thing!

There isn't a "podcast sheriff" that'll come to tell you you're breaking the rules.

Oh wait, yeah there is. That's me.

I'm the podcast sheriff. And I'm telling you not to launch your podcast until you have a plan.

Chapter 14: Launch Plan

CHAPTER 14: LAUNCH PLAN

"Okay, I think I've done everything for my podcast. Now do I just hit publish?"

Um, no. No, you do not. I mean, you can. You won't get thrown in podcast jail. There isn't a "podcast sheriff" that'll come to tell you you're breaking the rules. Oh wait, yeah there is. That's me. I'm the podcast sheriff. And I'm telling you *not* to launch your podcast until you have a plan. So, let's talk about your podcast launch goals, the plan you'll put in place, what you can expect on your podcast launch day and your first week, and the lessons I learned from launching.

Podcast Launch Goals: What to Aim For

Most people default to their overall podcast goals here. "I want to reach as many people as I can and impact the masses." That's a fantastic notion and one that I hope your podcast achieves one day. But right now, we're specifically talking about your podcast "launch" goals. Not your overall podcast goals.

WHAT ARE YOU TRYING TO ACCOMPLISH WITH YOUR PODCAST LAUNCH?

When you are clear about your goals, you can create a plan - with *specific* action steps - to get you there. In order to set up a proper plan, you have to know your destination. What are you aiming for? What does a successful launch look like to you? Start thinking about that as you develop a launch plan.

PODCAST LAUNCH GOALS TO CONSIDER

1. Reaching Apple's New & Noteworthy List

I feel like this is the highest goal most new podcasters shoot for. And while it's not impossible to achieve, there are some things that need to be in place first: You need an existing, *engaged* audience in order to make **New & Noteworthy** a for sure thing! This doesn't mean you can't reach this goal, but I want you to be realistic. If you're just starting out and you have ten people following you, the odds are not in your favor. It's not impossible, but you may have more legwork to do on the backend before you launch in order to get your show out there. Here's what that looks like:

- Growing your social media following.
- Growing your e-mail list.
- Growing your audience on a platform where you'll eventually share your podcast content.
- Setting clear expectations for your followers the day your podcast goes live:
  - Listen to all of the new episodes.
  - Leave a review.
  - Subscribe to the show.

2. Putting Your Content Out There

"I'm feeling a little nervous to put my stuff out there." I hear this a lot from my students, clients, and fellow podcasters. Everyone gets nervous around launch time. Because when you launch, that makes it real!

A real chance for people to hear what you've been working on. A real chance someone may listen to your podcast and *not* love it immediately. A real chance to put yourself out there and be vulnerable. A real chance *nobody* shows up to listen.

I get it. I've felt all of those emotions too. But if putting your content out there is what you need to do to prove to yourself that you can do it, then that should be your *only goal.* Put your content out there. Make it available for everyone else to see.

3. Being Consistent

If you need that accountability of knowing that people are waiting for you to put out your next episode, then consistency is your goal. I do really well with being held accountable, too. I like to know that there's a deadline to meet or someone waiting on me in order to light a fire under my rear. So, if being consistent is your main concern, then make that your number-one priority.

4. Achieving Certain Statistics

I don't want to talk about specific podcast launch goals for your first week's numbers, simply because I can't predict those...and neither can you. Not only that, but I don't find it helpful to call yourself a podcaster for downloads. Sure, it would be amazing to tell everyone, "You'll get a thousand downloads your first week, and I bet you'll hit a million by the end of your first year." But that's not how things have worked out for me, and there's a good chance that's not reality for you either.

Instead of dreaming and wondering about what your numbers will look like on launch day, I want you to go listen to *The Proffitt Podcast* Episode 70, "Podcast Growth, When Will I See It?" That's a good representation of how your show will develop over time and what you can expect to see as far as your podcast numbers go.

Now, I want you to pick a podcast launch goal. It doesn't have to be one of the goals we talked about here. It could be related to how many individual people you'll message that first week to tell them, "I launched my podcast! Go listen to it!" Or how many different cities you want to reach in your first month. Or any of a million other goals I haven't even thought of, but I want you to aim at something.

The Podcast Launch Plan

Can you hear yourself saying, "Oh. My. Goodness. Today is *launch day!!*"? Maybe you won't be that dramatic, but I remember saying those words like it was yesterday. Launch day is a special day. Except when I launched, I didn't have a great plan. In fact, I managed to create a pretty sad launch for my original podcast. I didn't have as many listeners as I'd hoped. The hype was distributed between myself and immediate members of my family, and I did a terrible job marketing my podcast launch. (Don't worry, I'll get into *all* the mistakes I made and things I wish I knew later in this chapter.)

In order to create a successful launch for your podcast, we need to discuss a few basic things. Then, before you know it, you'll be celebrating the first big milestone of your podcast! Sounds exciting, right?

In order to get the most out of everything we're about to cover, I need you to promise me that you'll work through each of the questions we're about to discuss. And then comes the hard part: you have to stick to the plan! Deal? Okay, let's do this!

PRO TIP: It helps to read through all the material in the next section before you really start to plan and implement your strategy. Most of these steps should be familiar by now anyway.

LET'S LAUNCH YOUR PODCAST THE RIGHT WAY!

1. CHOOSE YOUR PODCAST LAUNCH DATE

- What is a reasonable amount of time for you to get your podcast off the ground?
  - Six weeks? Six months? Next year? The time frame itself doesn't matter. It's about picking a realistic date that works for your schedule and then sticking to that date. Refer back to the podcast launch date you chose in Chapter 11.
- Mark your calendar, and hold firm on that date!
  - Make sure the date you choose to launch is at least three to four weeks from now.
- Like we said last chapter, you need at least seven to fourteen days to get connected to all of the platforms your podcast will appear on.
  - You also want a little time to maximize the impact of your launch.
- My Podcast Launch date is: _____
- How long is that from today? (Days/Weeks/Months) _____
- Does this time frame seem realistic? _____
- If not, why? _____
- NOTE: You don't have to have all of the details of your podcast worked out in order to pick your launch date. There may be some things you

are still working on or need to decide before you're really ready to launch. But don't wait until everything is "perfect." If you do, you'll never launch. Don't let a feeling of not being "ready" psyche you out. You got this!

2. ANNOUNCE YOUR PODCAST LAUNCH DATE

- This can be the scariest part of the whole launch, but you need to announce your launch date. (Why do you think Chapter 11 was dedicated to this?) Here are some ideas to recap how you can announce your podcast launch date:
  - Blast it all over social media
  - Tell your friends and family
  - Create a Facebook event
  - Tell strangers you meet at the store
  - Create graphics for launch day (Bonus points if you share those with friends to help you promote!)
  - Shout it from the rooftops

3. CONNECT TO PODCAST HOSTING SITE

- Find a podcast hosting service that works for you. (You already know I'm partial to Buzzsprout! They've been my go-to podcast hosting service since day one.) Remember, you need a little buffer room to get connected to all of the podcast directories through your hosting site. Plan accordingly for this when picking your podcast launch date.

4. LAUNCH WITH THREE TO FIVE EPISODES
- When listeners find a great podcast, they love to binge-listen to several episodes! I do it. You do it. And your future listeners will do it too! So, there are several good reasons to launch with multiple episodes:
  - Give your audience a taste of your personality.
  - Set expectations for what they will gain as a listener.
  - Launch your show with CTAs (calls-to-action) right out of the gate.
  - Choose the three to five episodes you'll launch with.

5. HOW WILL YOU PROMOTE THE LAUNCH OF YOUR PODCAST?
- Creating a "hype" party environment around your podcast is a great way to get people excited about your show. They'll want to cheer you on and share your content right out of the gate!

Here are some ideas to create an exciting environment for the launch of your podcast:

- ✓ Facebook events, live videos, posts, and groups
- ✓ Instagram stories, posts, IGTV, and lives
- ✓ YouTube Live and regular videos
- ✓ Announcement on website
- ✓ Media appearances (TV, radio)
- ✓ Sharing on interview guests' social media
- ✓ Sharing on interview guests' websites
- ✓ In-person launch-day event or happy hour
- ✓ E-mail sequence leading up to launch
- ✓ Promotion on other podcasts
- ✓ Guest posts on blogs
- ✓ Podcast-related giveaway
- ✓ Podcast sound bites and other teaser content

Circle the tools you'll use to create a party environment around your podcast launch date.

No matter how you decide to formulate and articulate your podcast launch plan, you want people to get excited about your podcast. Keep asking yourself the question, "How can I deliver more value?" Because that's what it's about: always delivering value to your audience!

What Do You Need to Be Ready on Your Podcast Launch Date?

I know that the podcast launch process will look different for different podcasters, but I wanted to give you a basic checklist to make sure you've done everything on your end to set your podcast launch up for success. (Check each box once it's complete.)

- ❑ Podcast cover artwork
- ❑ Three to five episodes completed and ready to upload
- ❑ Podcast connected to hosting site (seven to fourteen days to complete process)
- ❑ Trailer or first episode uploaded to hosting site
- ❑ Graphics to promote podcast launch online
- ❑ Social media account for podcast (optional)
- ❑ Website for podcast (optional)
- ❑ Announcement on website (optional)

The "optional" items literally could have kept flowing for another twenty pages, but I didn't want to overwhelm you. Once you have the basics down, then you can let the creative ideas kick into play.

What to Expect on Launch Day and Launch Week

Many of my students and clients ask me, "Okay, I've done all of this prep work for my launch plan, but what can I realistically expect to happen when I launch my podcast?" So, I'm excited to bring to you some real examples of what I experienced during my podcast launch.

10 Things I Wish I'd've Known Before I Launched

1. I should've launched with three or more episodes instead of just two!
- Two episodes didn't feel like enough to let listeners get a feel for my podcast. Especially since the first episode was my trailer, which was only seven minutes long.
- PRO TIP: Try for three to five episodes when you're launching. People will get to know you faster and learn what to expect each week and what kind of value you can offer them.

2. I should've researched my potential market more.
- I didn't know to see which days fit into their listening schedule or what they're really doing when they tune in. I also didn't know all the things I

told you to research and understand deeply back in Chapter 3 about your ideal listener.

- PRO TIP: Know your listeners. Know what they want to hear. Know why they're tuning in. Know what kind of value you can offer to them to make their lives better.

3. I needed to record more interviews or episodes before launching.

- When you don't plan ahead, creating content on the spot can be daunting, and I believe it's one of the main reasons new podcasters burn out quickly. I wish I had planned ahead and banked at least five more episodes before I launched to give myself more margin.
- PRO TIP: Always plan ahead! Try to have several episodes or interviews recorded before you launch. Or, at the very least, have those ideas planned out. If you haven't launched yet, plan time on your calendar now to make this happen!

4. I wish I'd had an entire month of episodes already scheduled from day one.

- If you can be proactive and get ahead, do it. At every stage. In every process. Try to have several more episodes recorded, edited, and cued up when you launch.

- PRO TIP: You can upload several episodes to your podcast hosting site and schedule them to be published later. Just be aware how much "air time" your hosting site plan allows.

5. The summer was a terrible time to launch my podcast.
- To have a podcast launch right in the middle of summer was bad timing. For a mom with three kids at home all summer, I was strapped for quiet, uninterrupted recording time. Content planning, getting ahead of schedule, and conducting interviews went on the back burner.
- PRO TIP: Choose a podcast launch date that works best for you *and* your audience. Pick a date, and then go all in!

6. My office echoes really badly!
- It's not the end of the world if you have bad acoustics in your environment. But don't ignore it. Find the best environment that you can to record.
- PRO TIP: You can record in a walk-in closet to minimize echo. Or slap some acoustic panels on the walls to deaden those echoes. But don't let bad audio drive listeners away!

7. I didn't sound so cheerful in my first few episodes.

- It's painful to go back and listen to some of the very first podcast episodes I did. Robotic. Monotone. And, dare I say it, a little boring. Don't be those things!
- PRO TIP: Always smile when you're recording!

8. I record better when I'm sitting or standing straight up.
- When I can move my hands and my arms naturally (without knocking the mic around), I speak better. Even if you have to use a Minecraft Creeper Head party box for a mic stand in the beginning (#truestory), use your resources to make yourself comfortable. Get scrappy!
- PRO TIP: Find what works best for you!

9. A lot of people still have *no clue* what a podcast is.
- It's amazing how many people still don't know what a podcast is or how to access them. And that's okay. They don't know what they don't know.
- PRO TIP: Learn how to tell people where to find your podcast without making them look or feel dumb. Those who don't know will appreciate your efforts and trust you more!

10. I wish I had promoted my show more in the first few weeks.

- Let's be real here, I didn't have a great launch plan. Therefore, my show didn't have as great of a launch as I had hoped for, which is why everything I've shared with you in this chapter is a result of what I *wish* I had done!
- PRO TIP: Spend some time developing a great podcast launch plan. The strategies you implement can greatly increase the momentum your podcast has from the very beginning!

11. **BONUS TIP:** Ask listeners to subscribe and leave a review on day one!

- Start implementing calls-to-action (CTAs) on day one! Even if you're just asking for a social media follow, a website visit, or a subscription wherever they're tuning in, ask listeners to engage with you from the very beginning.
- PRO TIP: I know it can feel awkward at first, but it starts feeling more natural the more you do it. So, start engaging on day one!

Here's the Bottom Line

I want you to do what's going to work for you. I wanted to give you some ideas for all of the ways you can promote the fact that you're starting a podcast, but if the ideas don't work or don't feel right, get creative. Come up with something else. But do something.

Because if you don't promote it, then how are people ever going to know that it's there?

You can't depend on someone to type the exact name of your podcast on the exact date that your podcast is going to launch and hope that they find you. That's not a good strategy. We're in this to find our listeners and bring value to them.

And remember one more thing: it doesn't have to be perfect. But you do have to put it out there to start seeing what is going to work. I know it's scary, but you can totally do this. You got this!

Krystal Proffitt

Content teasers are exactly what they sound like: ways to get your audience interested and curious about your content. You want people saying, "Ohhh, I want to know more about that!"

You're teasing them.

Offering them a little taste of your amazing content.

Chapter 15: Content Teasers

CHAPTER 15: CONTENT TEASERS

Can we just take a sec to celebrate all that you've learned up to this point? You've named your podcast, found your ideal listener, created some content ideas, maybe recorded some episodes (or at least played around with your equipment), and gotten serious about launching. You may have even launched your podcast by now! And that deserves a few pats on the back, some hootin' and hollerin', and some celebrating, because you are doing it. You're officially podcasting!

But just when the excitement dies down and the newness wears off a little, you start to ask yourself, "How am I supposed to keep talking about my podcast without bugging the crap out of everyone?" Well, let me introduce you to *content teasers*.

What Are Content Teasers?

Did you ever watch the 1990s Sylvester Stallone movie *Cliffhanger*? Stallone's character is a mountain climber, and the opening scene is of a helicopter flying through the mountains looking for the courageous Stallone as he tries to rescue a pair of climbers stranded on top of a steep peak. I won't spoil it for you in case you want to watch it later, but it's literally the definition of a cliffhanger. You want to know what happens next. You are on the edge of your seat trying to figure out what happened. That's what you're trying to accomplish with your podcast. And that can happen when you tease your content.

Content teasers are exactly what they sound like: ways to get your audience interested and curious about your content. You want people saying, "Ohhh, I want to know more about that!" You're teasing them. Offering them a little taste of your amazing content.

Here are some examples of the content teasers that have worked for me, as both a content creator and consumer of lots of podcasts!

Sound Bites or Audiograms

These are short clips of your upcoming podcast episodes that are designed to pique listeners' interest ahead of the air dates.

The obvious question is, "How do you create these?" There are several platforms that help podcasters design and create these sound bites and audiograms, but for the sake of simplicity, I'm going to tell you what I've used.

- Buzzsprout's "Create a Video Sound Bite" Option
  - This is available to Buzzsprout users and can be accessed directly within each episode. This is not an additional cost, but just another

added benefit of being part of the Buzzsprout platform.

- Headliner
  - As of publishing this book, Headliner offers ten unwatermarked videos per month on their free plan.

I've used both platforms regularly to promote my podcast, and I know it's something that helps remind my listeners when new episodes are out. But as a listener of podcasts, I appreciate when other podcasters put these out too! I get excited when I see Amy Porterfield post in her Instagram Stories a short clip of the audio. I'm already an avid listener subscribed to her podcast, but I'm also a busy entrepreneur. Sometimes I need that reminder to listen to the next episode so I don't fall behind. (And if you haven't already, you need to run to the *Online Marketing Made Easy* podcast and subscribe. Immediately! I'm not kidding. Put this book down and go. I'll wait. Because Amy gives the best tips, strategies, advice, and stories. Plus, she's an online rock star!)

What to Include in a Sound Bite?

This can change from show to show. Some people name-drop, including audio from celebrity guests so their audience is more likely to listen. Some people include a hook that entices audiences to figure out what it is that they are talking about. If you've done all the planning and you know your content ahead of time, then you could post your hook on social media. When I was doing *The Rookie Life*, I did an episode with someone who was held at gunpoint. (Umm, yeah! Crazy story!) I used that sound bite from the episode to grab my listeners' attention.

You can also use the sound bite to focus on one of the important questions you ask during the interview. Your listeners will be interested to find out the answer to that specific question. But this really goes back to knowing your audience. What do they want to hear? And how do they want information delivered to them?

I did an interview once with Kayla Olson, author of the young adult books *The Sandcastle Empire* and *This Splintered Silence*, who sold the rights to *The Sandcastle Empire* to Leonardo DiCaprio. Yes, Jack from *Titanic*. (He totally could have fit on that door, Rose!) Kind of a big deal, right? I can't wait to see her book turned into a movie. Truly incredible! And that's how I teased that episode. Leonardo DiCaprio was an attention-grabbing name.

Videos

I get it. You're a podcaster. You didn't sign up to do videos, right? They make you uncomfortable. You don't like seeing yourself on camera. If you wanted to make videos all of the time, you would've gone the YouTube route, right? I understand. It may not be your favorite, but it's incredibly important these days.

People connect with our voices, but they also want to see our faces and know that we're actual human beings. Just think for a second about some of the brands you follow. Do you connect more with the ones you see on a regular basis? (You're nodding your head "Yes," right?) Of course, you do. It's the same with a podcast!

I'm not saying you have to commit to going live on social media every single day, but one to two live videos per week can help you create even deeper connections with your audience. You can create these videos on Facebook Live, InstaStories, YouTube, TikTok, or wherever your listeners are hanging out! And here are a few ideas for what you can include:

- Behind the scenes details
- Clips of interviews in progress
- Your editing processes
- Planning new content
- Upcoming topics
- What's new on the podcast

Personally, I love live video! But I didn't always love it. I was self-conscious about looking great. I was nervous I'd have a piece of lettuce stuck in my teeth.

And I still get the nervous sweats before I go live on someone else's page or talk about something for the very first time. But the first most part, I've fully embraced video, because that's where the future is headed. Plus, it's a great way to get in front of your audience. It puts a face to the podcaster, and it lets people connect with you on a different level.

Posting Graphics with Your Episode Descriptions

It's also useful to post graphics with your episode hook. I really like to get creative here and try new things all the time! But if you find something that works well for you right out of the gate, stick with what your audience resonates with most. Graphics give you and your brand a real opportunity to stand out and shine, identifying yourself and your show. People start to recognize colors, fonts, and symbols and associate them with your brand. (I can recognize a Starbucks logo from five miles down the highway. That green mermaid woman is like a beacon to me because they've done so well with their branding!)

CANVA.COM

We briefly talked about Canva when we were discussing your podcast artwork, but I use it on a daily basis! Whether I'm creating graphics to promote the podcast, my latest YouTube video, or another marketing graphic for my website, I'm constantly using this amazing graphic design tool. But I don't create from scratch every time. Oh, no, no. I've created a template with my brand colors, my fonts, and my podcast name, and I work from that each time I create a graphic. Don't reinvent the wheel. Create a template. Save time and headaches! Here are some of the ways I use graphics for the podcast:

- Promoting new episodes
- Teasing guest interviews
- Posting to Pinterest
- Quoting episodes
- Making announcements
- Teasing future content
- And so much more!

WRITING SOCIAL MEDIA POSTS: REPURPOSING PODCAST DESCRIPTIONS

If you hate writing for social media, I'm about to blow your mind! I copy the exact words from my podcast episode descriptions and use those alongside my graphics and sound bites to promote my episodes on social media! Yup, I hope I just blew your mind! There's no need to rack your brain trying to figure out what you're going to say to promote each episode. You've already done the work. Now, grab a video or graphic, copy your episode description, throw some emojis in there, and promote it on your favorite platforms!

Using Content Teasers on Social Media

I want you to feel confident in whichever marketing strategies you use for your podcast. But, let's be real. Technology is changing so quickly these days that what I mention here, right now, in this book may be totally different in six months. So instead of specific ways to "hack the algorithm" or get your info in front of more people, I wanted to give you some questions to consider as you create your social media strategy.

- Why are you posting on social?
  - Are you trying to engage your audience?
  - Are you trying to get them to listen to your podcast on a specific platform?
- What value are you offering?
  - Is there an amazing insight they'd gain from listening to your episode?
  - Does your interview have a rock star guest you know will blow their mind?
- What is your number one call-to-action for each post?
  - Do you want people to listen to the podcast on a certain podcast player?

- Do you want to make sure they grab the free download you're offering in the episode?
- Do you share information about a time-sensitive event, program, training, etc. in the episode they need to know about?
- Are you going to ask people to share your content or tell others to listen?

Building an E-mail List for Your Podcast

Another thing that you can do is send e-mails with teaser content, where you share the hook of your episode. You could also include a graphic or screenshot of you conducting your interview. However you shape it, the point is to really utilize your e-mail list for promoting your podcast episodes.

"How are you supposed to grow you e-mail list with a podcast?" Do you already have an e-mail list? Do you know why it's important to have an e-mail list? Well, I can't get into *all* things e-mail here because this is not my expertise. But I've learned some things along my journey. The biggest takeaway is the ability to access your audience *without* social media. Especially since we've seen the way social media tends to have a mind of its own from time to time. (People absolutely lose their minds if it's down for too long!)

HOW DO YOU SHARE YOUR PODCAST WITH YOUR E-MAIL LIST?

That is a great question. There are a few ways to do this, but one of my favorites is to share the link in the "P.S." of my weekly e-mail newsletter. I send out an e-mail to my list every Friday, no matter what. I publish multiple pieces of content throughout the week, but instead of bombarding my subscribers every time there's a new piece of content, I just add that week's content in the "P.S." at the bottom. It's less invasive to the people who actually want to read what's in the e-mail and easier for those who just want links to the content. Win-Win! To share your podcast content at the bottom of your e-mails, you can link directly to your website if you upload your podcast episodes there or to Apple Podcast, Google Play, Stitcher, Spotify, or wherever you want your audience to listen.

SEND AN E-MAIL THE DAY A NEW EPISODE AIRS

If you want to learn from the master of building e-mail lists, Amy Porterfield is your girl. She is the host of the *Online Marketing Made Easy* podcast, and she sends some of the *best* e-mails. In her weekly e-mails, she shares a specific part of her latest episode that she knows will draw attention. Or she shares a personal "aha" moment or takeaway she learned from her guest.

When she sends out her weekly newsletter, she includes the new information for the podcast, linked directly to her website. From there, you can listen to the podcast, download whatever freebies she's offering, and click any additional resources related to the podcast.

There are many ways to do this, but I highly recommend that you start an e-mail list for your podcast...immediately!

STEPS TO GROWING AN E-MAIL LIST WITH A PODCAST

I did a talk in October 2019 for PodHouston, the largest community of podcasters in the Houston area, and we talked about growing your e-mail list with a podcast. You can check out the YouTube video for some visuals, but I'll explain the gist of it here.

1. Create a Freebie
   - This needs to be something that can solve a problem for your listeners or that offers valuable advice.
   - You can create anything from a free PDF to a video, audio file, etc. but it needs to be something of value to your ideal listeners.
2. Build a Landing Page
   - What's the purpose of the landing page? A place for value exchange.

- ○ It's where your potential subscriber has the opportunity to see what you have to offer (your value to them) in exchange for their e-mail address (the value given to you - their trust).
- ○ How to format your landing page
  - Name your freebie clearly
  - Speak to their pain points (problems)
  - Call out who your freebie is for
  - Keep it simple!
3. Create a Thank You Page
   - ○ Your Thank You page is another opportunity to build trust and authority!
   - ○ There are two ways to craft your Thank You Page:
     - With a website
       - Have an opportunity to further the relationship with your listener/subscriber
       - Use videos, links to social media, or your top resources to add even more value
     - Without a website
       - You're limited to what your message can show
       - But take advantage of being able to connect with your

audience on as many levels as
possible

4. Develop a Welcome Sequence
   - What is a welcome sequence?
     - A sequence of e-mails a new
       subscriber receives once they've opted
       in to your freebie. It usually includes
       three to five e-mails, delivers the
       freebie, introduces you and/or your
       podcast, offers advice, and gives
       resources.
     - These are simply a few ideas and
       suggestions to get you started with
       your e-mail sequence. Don't feel like
       you have to include them all.
   - Why is a welcome sequence important?
     - It gives you a chance to further your
       relationship with a brand-new
       subscriber. You don't want to be a
       "one-hit wonder" - you want to be
       their go-to expert!
   - What should a welcome sequence include?
     - Freebie delivery
     - Welcome/Intro
     - Testimonies or stories of how you've
       helped others or achieved success in
       your industry

- Resources
5. Deliver a URL as Your Call-to-Action
    - All you need to announce on your podcast is where listeners can grab the freebie you've created just for them - a URL. The URL either be the landing page or a page with an opt-in form.
    - Here are a few examples:
        - "If you need content ideas for your podcast, I encourage you to grab my *free* 500+ Podcast Ideas for Any Industry at KrystalProffitt.com/500podcastideas."
        - "If you're looking to launch a podcast, grab my Basic Podcast Launch Plan at KrystalProffitt.com/launch."

PRO TIP: make your calls-to-action very clear within your podcast episodes. Get people to join your e-mail list through your podcast. This doesn't mean you have to say "go join my e-mail newsletter," though you can if you want. But I'd love to see you create and offer a lead magnet or freebie that is directly related to your podcast topic. Share that valuable info you have so that people want to join your e-mail list. For example, I advertise my free download, "500+ Podcast Ideas (for Any Industry)." I have a clip within the show that tells people exactly where they can go to grab this workbook so they never run out of podcast ideas! You can do the exact same thing with your lead magnet.

Incorporate Promotional Content into Your Podcast Calendar

Okay, let's talk about you incorporating all of these ideas into your content calendar. Look at what day or days of the week you're going to publish your podcast. When should you tease it? Probably the day of or the day before. Put something out into the world saying, "Hey, this episode is out there. Here's where you can find it, go check it out." That will create consistency. People will start to recognize your podcast and your podcast brand, and they'll start to have responses like, "Oh, here's a new graphic and sound bite. That must mean there's a new podcast episode." That's what you're looking for. You're looking for that trigger that will make people want to go listen to what you have to say.

Now, here is your mission: Go play around with some of these content teasers. Maybe you love some of these. Maybe you hate some. And maybe some of them just aren't going to work for you. But I encourage you to try a few of these out as you start marketing your podcast and see what's going to work for you and what's not. Now that you've got some ideas on how to market your podcast, let's talk about the ways you can continue to learn more about your audience, what they want to hear, and how you can deliver as much value as possible.

Krystal Proffitt

I'm obsessed with understanding my audience. Not in a creepy way! In a way that shows how much I care and want to deliver value to them every week.

Chapter 16: Survey Your Audience

CHAPTER 16: SURVEY YOUR AUDIENCE

I was asked recently, "How can you understand your audience better? Like, actually get to know them and what they want?" I thought it was a trick question, and I pray that my answer wasn't totally off putting. "You ask them…" I know, I felt smart-alecky as it came out of my mouth, but that's the truth. You have to ask your audience what kind of content they want to hear. And surveying your audience on a regular basis is one of the best ways to ensure that you continue to deliver value and stay relevant.

We're going to talk about surveying your audience and getting feedback on what you're creating to keep the momentum going. Make sure you keep delivering amazing content to your audience, because if you just start throwing stuff out there and it's not resonating with anyone, then you're really not going to get that traction.

Ways to Survey Your Audience

When you think of a "survey" there's a good chance you picture someone with a clipboard asking boring questions like, "First name? Age? Date of Birth?

Height? Weight? What do you do for a living?" and the process continues for the next seven years of your life. That's *not* what we're talking about when I say *survey*. There are tons of ways to get feedback from your audience! And the ways I engage with my audience are constantly changing. Not only am I trying to keep up with the latest technology and trendy platforms, but my audience is evolving, too. As they learn and discover what I'm teaching them on the podcast, they want more. They want new information or a different spin on an old topic, or they want to hear from new guests or learn about new resources to explore. How do I know? Because I ask. I'm *obsessed* with understanding my audience. Not in a creepy way! In a way that shows how much I care and want to deliver value to them every week. Here are a few of the ways I survey my audience:

- Ask in a Facebook group
    - You can ask questions in a Facebook group you've created for your podcast, or you could find other groups related to your podcast topic or where your ideal listener hangs out online. Pay attention to where your audience is.
    - If it's your Facebook community, you can keep your survey or questions simple and direct. "Hey y'all. What else do you want me

to talk about on the podcast? I'm coming up with content ideas and would love your input."

- ○ If you're asking questions in someone else's group, don't be the spammy person. Tell them from the beginning of the post, "Hey everyone. I'm doing research for some future podcast content and I wanted to know..." Be honest, answer every comment, and always offer value. You're not trying to bait and switch people to listen to your podcast or buy something from you. You're trying to understand your audience better. And when you genuinely talk to people to try to understand them better, they have a tendency to open up to you.

- Tease content to test engagement
  - ○ You don't have to share your entire content calendar. But if you want to make sure you're on the right track, I'd challenge you to be bold and share your next five to ten episode ideas. Ask people, "Which topics are you *most* excited to hear about next month?"
  - ○ If you've spent some time developing a relationship with your people - the people who are a "right fit" for your podcast and its content - then they'll tell you what they want.

- ○ Word of caution: it may not always be what you want to hear. They may come back with, "None of those sound exciting." Or, "Oh, I thought you already covered that. Can you cover this topic instead?" Don't ignore that feedback! And don't take it as criticism. They are giving you insanely important clues to follow on your path to more downloads, more shares, and more satisfied listeners.
- Conduct polls on Facebook
  - ○ In order to create a poll on Facebook, create a post, select "Add to Your Post," and select the "Poll" feature. You can add pictures or GIFs to make the poll more noticeable and engaging. You can use some of the survey questions listed in the Google Forms survey section below, but I suggest you use language that's relevant to your audience so they'll be more likely to answer you and connect with the questions you're asking.
  - ○ I don't *love* creating polls on Facebook, only because you don't get notified when people make a selection. (At least, that's how it is as of printing this book.) So, you could take time to create the perfectly crafted survey for your audience - something that would be of great value to you and your podcast - but

unless you "save" the poll, the information gets lost. I mean, technically it doesn't just disappear, but you have to go back into the group or your page or wherever you posted the poll and find it. Plus, the "Choose an Option" kind of survey isn't always as engaging as open-ended questions.

- Conduct polls on Instagram Stories
  - There's an awesome feature within Instagram stories that I love to use called "Poll." It's exactly what it sounds like: it polls your audience. You can give people two options: A or B, peanut butter or jelly, rap or country, ridiculous or corny, yes or no. You can literally poll your audience with any question that comes to your imagination, but you're limited on the number of characters your answers can be. I like to ask simple questions that involve a single emoji—maybe a happy face versus a sad or mad face for how your toddler makes you feel when they spill their full cup of milk all over the kitchen. I know, it's a silly example, but it is a fun way to engage my audience on Instagram. Does this have anything to do with my podcast? No, but it brings my audience behind the scenes with me and who

I am as a mom. You could ask people, "Which topic do you want to hear me talk about next?" And then give them two options. The possibilities are endless here, and I love how creative you can get.

- Create an actual survey with Google Forms
  - If you want to go all in and take the "survey your audience" idea very literally, you can create a survey with Google Forms. There are other platforms out there that create "quiz-like" surveys, but Google Forms is the one I default to. You could send a survey like this to your audience at least two to three times per year to make sure you're on the right track.
  - I've created more than ten different surveys that I send to clients, students, and potential members of my community whenever I have a new idea, but I think simple is better. You don't want your audience bogged down with confusing questions and a survey that looks like it may never end. Instead, start with ten questions as kind of a "Getting to Know Your Audience" type of survey. Here are some questions you can tailor to your podcast topic:

1. What are you struggling with right now?
2. What do you want to know more about?
3. Where have you gone to find this information previously?
4. What has been the most impactful piece of content you consumed lately?
5. What books are you currently reading?
6. What are your top three favorite podcasts?
7. When/where do you listen to my podcast?
8. What is your favorite thing about [insert your podcast topic]?
9. What is your least favorite thing about [insert your podcast topic]?
10. You can throw in some demographic questions to help you further qualify your listeners and who they are.

- Talk to people at in-person events
  - Does your industry have conferences or other in-person events you can attend? That's a good place to survey people. Not with a clipboard or voice recorder, but informally. Connect with your ideal listener in real life

whenever possible. Ask people, "What do you think about [insert podcast topic]?" or "What do you think is missing from the marketplace that I could potentially share on my podcast?"

PROTIP: You can also find other successful podcasters in your industry and see who their audience is. (Podcast modeling once again!) Do some research on what topics they cover. This isn't necessarily surveying your audience, but it's more about being observant of what's going on in the industry and paying attention to what's happening.

WHEN TO SEND A SURVEY

Don't survey your audience too much. Just like with e-mail or social media or calls or texts or any other type of communication, there's a balance. But how often should you survey your audience? Well, I'll give you a good example. Let's say you found one episode that was really a homerun, right? You found yourself saying, "Holy moly! I had three times more downloads for this one episode than I did for the last five combined!" Pay attention to those things. That's a fantastic time to follow those clues and the breadcrumbs that lead to future success for other episodes.

And the best way you capitalize on a homerun piece of content is to ask your audience, "What did you like about that particular episode? (Or post or video or whatever?)" That way, you can create more content just like that. We've covered this a little bit throughout the book, but I want to make sure that this concept really sinks in. You'll find the balance for what works for you and your audience as time goes on—whether surveying needs to be done on a daily, weekly, or monthly basis will be determined by how engaged you are with your audience and how often you feel like you need to make that connection with them.

HOW I SEND SURVEYS

Now that I've been podcasting for a while, I feel comfortable asking my audience all kinds of questions. "Did you like that episode? What was your biggest takeaway? Did you find value in the freebie that went with that episode?" And my listeners feel more appreciated when I create content that directly answers the questions they have. Plus, I want to deliver content that's going to make their lives easier or help them with their podcast journey. That's the whole purpose of my podcast—to help and serve others.

So, connect with your audience. Your mission should be to understand your audience on a level that makes creating content easier, makes marketing your podcast a piece of cake, and knocks the socks off of your people! Lead with value, and follow it up with a good survey!

Krystal Proffitt

If you can explain your podcast to a ten-year-old and they fully understand it, success!

If not, go back to the drawing board.

Something isn't clear.

Chapter 17: Elevator Pitch

CHAPTER 17: ELEVATOR PITCH

Of all the elements of podcasting, this has to be the one I have the strongest love-hate relationship with. Crafting an elevator pitch was something I struggled with for a really, really long time. When I started *The Rookie Life*, I wanted to create a short video on my website to preview the show and its purpose. Let me tell you, even with the words scripted out on a giant whiteboard, I struggled getting them out. "My show is called *The Rookie Life*, and I talk about, ummm…and it might be for women, all women. No, business women, no…female entrepreneurs. And we share stories. And, um, stories that are relatable. And can inspire you."

I can just imagine someone stumbling upon that video and thinking, "Um, I don't understand. Who is this podcast for? What is she talking about? What kind of stories? Am I one of the business women she's talking to? None of this sounds interesting. I'll just listen to something else—anything else—instead." My message was not clear.

So, if this is a struggle for you, you're not alone. And if you've never created an elevator pitch before, then this might be a little challenging. But I'm sharing some tools and resources to make this process so much easier.

What Is an Elevator Pitch?

First things first: what the heck is an elevator pitch? If you're not familiar with that term, it's what people use to describe a situation where you're prompted to tell someone what you're all about in the time it takes to ride an elevator. Picture this: you're in an elevator with someone, the ride could last anywhere from thirty to sixty seconds), and they say, "So, what do you do?"

Your default may be what mine used to be: a deer-in-headlights reaction. That's awkward, but it's also the reality you'll be faced with if you haven't prepared for such a moment. Let me give you another scenario that doesn't involve strangers on elevators.

Imagine you're at a dinner party. Your friends and family members know that you've recently started your podcast. Or, at the very least, you're thinking about it. Someone, let's say Aunt Sally, walks up to you. You haven't seen each other since Uncle Bob's last birthday. She gives you a big ol' hug and says, "Hey, how's it going? What have you been up to lately?" Well, of course, the first thing you're talking about is your podcast, right?

So, you deliver your elevator pitch that's perfectly crafted for such a moment. Aunt Sally probably looks at you funny because she doesn't fit into your ideal listener audience, but she responds with, "Well, that's nice hun."

This scenario never went down exactly this way for me. I never got a "that's nice hun." Instead, after five minutes trying to explain what my show was about, I got confused looks from my brothers' friends at our kids' birthday parties. "Your podcast is about what?" my brother asked me. It took me forever to spit it out, and my message was still unclear. That's not going to be your story, though. And it's not mine anymore!

Questions to Answer for Your Elevator Pitch

As uncomfortable as any of those scenarios may be, let's break down some of the questions you should be prepared to answer. Some of these are obvious and simple. Some take a while to articulate, which is why we're doing this exercise.

- What's the name of your show?
- What's it about?
- Who's it for?
- When do new episodes come out?
- How can it add value to your listeners?
- Why should I listen?

All of these are questions I was asked in the first months of my show. Sometimes I could answer them on the spot. Other times, I felt like a complete idiot. On the surface, these questions look so simple, but if you don't have the answers, you'll have a tough time marketing your podcast.

I heard somewhere that you should craft your elevator pitch so a fourth grader can understand. If you can explain your podcast to a ten-year-old and they fully understand it, success! If not, go back to the drawing board. Something isn't clear. Maybe it's your wording. It could be the order of your message.

ANSWER THE RIGHT QUESTIONS

Take some time. Don't rush this exercise. Because if you do, you're not going to remember what you said. Also, this takes practice. You won't have your pitch memorized right after you script a few sentences. So, start practicing. Start saying it to people. Start with people you know if you feel a little embarrassed or you don't feel like you quite have it yet. Say it to your dog. Say it to your kids. Say it to your partner. Say it to someone who is not going to judge you. Say it to someone who's supportive of your podcasting journey. Practice it over and over until you really get it down.

Some Rules to Follow

"I help people with confidence and motivation to ensure that they're fully confident and motivated to achieve their greatest desires and overcome the deterrents that hold them back from their inner impediments that control their viability in the tranquil beings that they are."

What the…what? No. No. No. Don't use language that is cutesy or confusing. Stop it. Instead, find a clear and concise way to deliver your elevator pitch. Here, I'll share mine:

Hi, I'm Krystal Proffitt, and I host The Proffitt Podcast. I teach entrepreneurs how to confidently start, launch, and market their podcasts. We publish episodes every Tuesday and Thursday and cover everything from equipment to content development to how to deliver the most value to your audience.

And that's my elevator pitch. A ten-year-old can understand it. Even if you have a podcast that uses technical language, I encourage you to frame it in a way that is very simple and concise, not confusing, so anyone on the street could ask you what you do and you could explain it to them.

"If You Confuse, You Lose"

I told you earlier about one of the best business books I've ever read: *Building a Story Brand,* by Donald Miller. I heard him a few years ago on a podcast. I knew his name. I'd heard a little about who he was, but it wasn't until I read his book that I could fully appreciate his work and what he teaches business owners.

In a nutshell, his organization focuses on bringing story to life. "I'll ruin every movie for you after I teach what I know about story," I remember him saying that in the podcast interview. And it's true. Now any time I sit down with my husband, Seth, to watch a movie, I can spy the villain and know how the story is most likely going to end before we run out of popcorn. Miller's story framework works like a gem. But what does it have to do with podcasting? Everything.

Whether you plan to monetize your podcast (which we'll talk about in the next chapter) or not, you need to be able to talk to your listeners. Not only identifying who your ideal customer is, but connecting with them on a deeper level. Miller has coined the phrase, "If you confuse, you lose," and those words reverberate through my mind anytime I sit down to plan any piece of content for my podcast.

"No, I can't talk about podcast's backend statistics without first explaining why they're important. I don't need to go into five different topics in one episode because the message will be diluted. I need to focus on keeping it simple and not confusing." If you confuse, you lose.

And this advice applies to your elevator pitch, as well.

I want you to take Miller's phrase, write it on a sticky note, and hang it up somewhere around your workspace. Read it every time you start to craft an e-mail to someone. Say it out loud before you hit record. Let this message sink into your being as you continue on this podcast journey. But most importantly, repeat it over and over again as you practice your elevator pitch. Here's a quick practice:

- Say your pitch out loud.
  - Ask yourself, "Was any part of it confusing?"
- Say it to someone else.
  - Ask them, "Was any of it confusing?"
- Say your pitch to your neighbor's ten-year-old daughter.
  - Was she confused when you finished?

If at any point you run into confusion, stop and try again. I know, it seems like a lot of work for such a small piece of the puzzle. But it matters. If you can't talk about your podcast, how are you going to be able to invite big guests on to your show? How will you be able to pitch your podcast to potential sponsors? How will you be able to explain it to Aunt Sally at the next family get together? Take your time. Do it right. It will pay off.

When to Use Your Elevator Pitch

We've spent a lot of time crafting your elevator pitch and understanding its role in marketing your podcast, but now let's talk about the practical ways you'll use your pitch over the lifetime of your podcast.

PODCAST GUESTS

In Chapter 7, we talked about your podcast show guidelines. This is a great place to throw in your elevator pitch. One clear, concise explanation of what your podcast is all about, who it's for, and why it matters can make a huge difference for a podcast guest who's deciding whether your show is a right fit for them.

POTENTIAL SPONSORS

There are many factors that go into approaching potential podcast sponsors, but one of the most important should be your elevator pitch. Whether you meet with a potential sponsor in-person, over the phone, through e-mail, or through a private message on social media, how you talk about your podcast is important. You don't want to be confusing about your topic, and they will want to know exactly who your target audience is. You need to feel confident going into the conversation that you have all of that information in one place.

POTENTIAL LISTENERS

I love a good business conference. I know that's super nerdy to say, but I don't really care. I love a good networking event where like-minded people who are motivated and on fire for self-improvement get together to talk about world domination...or the latest in podcast trends. (Same thing, right?) But I've found that when you attend these events two questions come up: 1. Where are you from? 2. What do you do?

People aren't usually shocked that I'm from Texas (because of the accent), but when I tell them with confidence and clarity that I teach entrepreneurs how to start, launch, and market their podcasts, one or two things happen. They either perk up with their shoulders back and say, "I've always wanted to have a podcast!" Or they say, "Oh, I need to tell my friend about you! She was just saying she wanted to start a podcast." Maybe the conferences I attend are just filled with potential podcasters, or maybe podcasting really is that popular nowadays—either way, good for me! — but I no longer get blanks stares or responses like, "What? I don't understand."

So, use your elevator pitch any time someone asks about your podcast. You may be rocky at first, but that's why I want you to practice and practice and practice some more. It'll be easy to recite before you know it.

*There are tons of
opportunities to make money
with a podcast, but you have to
have two things before you can
make it a reality:
patience and strategy.*

Chapter 18: Monetization

CHAPTER 18: MONETIZATION

"Is there any money to be made in the podcasting world? I've done everything I need to do to create my podcast. But realistically, how can I make money? Do I need millions of downloads before I actually see any return on this investment of my time, money, and energy?"

Maybe these have been the questions you've had since you first picked up this book. The answers are, yes, there is money to be made, and no, you don't have to have millions of downloads before you start to see cash coming in for your podcast. But you do have to be smart and strategic from the beginning if you want to reap the rewards of a successful podcast for years to come. There are tons of opportunities to make money with a podcast, but you have to have two things before you can make it a reality: patience and strategy. And if you're anything like me, you just rolled your eyes reading the word "patience."

Many of us start something and want to see results immediately, or yesterday, but that will rarely be the case when it comes to making money with your podcast. So instead of teaching you the traditional way of attracting advertising dollars to your podcast through millions of downloads, I want to talk about ways to make money with your podcast from day one.

Five Ways to Make Money Podcasting

Not all ways of making money with a podcast are created equal. You may choose to try one or all of these at some point over the life of your podcast, but I advise starting with the strategy that makes the most sense for you and your audience. I'll go into more detail for each strategy in a second, but first let's break down the five ways to make money with your podcast:

1. Affiliate marketing
2. Listener-sponsored membership sites
3. Selling your own services
4. Selling merchandise
5. Selling products, programs, or events

Now, let's dive into the nitty-gritty of each strategy.

1. Affiliate Marketing

"How can I make money on day one of my podcast?"

This is usually the question I see once new podcasters have gotten their groove or if they're trying to decide whether the podcast journey is going to be for them. What I typically tell people is, "If you're brand new to an online platform, start with affiliate marketing. It's the easiest place to get started, and it doesn't require a ton of work on your part." But how does it actually work?

Affiliate marketing is sharing a specific URL that's exclusive to you in some way. Whenever anybody clicks that URL and then makes a purchase, you get a small kickback. I've been a part of many affiliate programs where they give you a version of their main website followed by a unique identifying number or name, like: *www.krystalproffitt.com/affiliate1234*

The easiest place to get started with affiliate marketing is Amazon. Why? Because you can literally buy anything on Amazon. If there are products or books or anything related to your podcast/industry/business/hobby/etc. that can be purchased on Amazon, then I suggest finding those and recommending them on your podcast.

HOW DO YOU SET UP AN AFFILIATE LINK FOR YOUR PODCAST?

Once you've setup an affiliate account with Amazon (or another affiliate program), you can start to share the link with your audience and other members of your podcast community. You can place them in your episode descriptions, the show notes on your website, posts on your social media, or wherever else you'd like.

Disclaimer: I want to make sure that this is very clear: you MUST follow the Federal Trade Commission's (FTC) regulations when it comes to affiliate marketing. You must disclose that the link you're providing is an affiliate link and that you will have monetary gain when anyone makes a purchase through that link. You can find more information on the proper guidelines and regulations at FTC.gov.

For podcast episodes related to any affiliate programs, I put the link in my show notes with a disclaimer at the top of the page. "[This post contains affiliate links. If a purchase is made, I may receive a small commission at no extra cost to you.]" That's my disclaimer and how I like to inform people who visit my website that they're about to click on an affiliate link. Again, you must properly disclose any and all affiliate links.

OTHER AFFILIATE PROGRAMS

Like I said earlier, there are tons of programs that you could be an affiliate for, but I wanted to give you some real-life examples in case you wanted to try any of these out for yourself.

Podcast Hosting Site

If you're a Buzzsprout customer, they offer the "Refer a Friend" program. You can send your unique account link (which you'll find within your Buzzsprout account) to friends and family. If they switch to a paid account through your link, you'll receive an Amazon gift card for your referral. You may not make millions doing this, but any time I get an e-mail from Buzzsprout saying I have a $25 gift card waiting for me, I get excited!

Buzzsprout also rolled out their "Affiliate Marketplace" program, which can be found in the Podcast Monetization section of your account. This includes companies that have been vetted to have great products, offer exclusive deals for Buzzsprout users, pay in cash, and don't set a barrier to entry based on how many downloads you have. You can get started immediately!

E-mail Service Provider (ESP)

If you have an online business of any kind, it's likely that you also use an e-mail service provider. I've been using ConvertKit.com since November 2018 and have been an affiliate for just as long. Why? Because I believe in their platform. I love using their program and don't have a problem at all telling someone who's shopping for an e-mail service provider to choose them. Plus, I tell podcasters all the time how much they need an e-mail list!

So, I share my affiliate link with anyone who asks about a good ESP. And if they sign up through my link, great. I get a credit toward my account. If they don't, that's okay too.

Tools and Products You Love

There is a planner I've used for two years now called "The LivingWell Planner." The creator of the product is someone I've followed for several years, and when she announced she was going to have an affiliate program, I hopped on board. "Why not," I asked myself. "I mean, I love the product. I already tell people about it. Why not make a little extra cash by telling others to use it, too?" Look into affiliate opportunities that you can use for your podcast, your business, or any other part of your journey.

2. Listener-Sponsored Membership Sites

What in the world are listener-sponsored membership sites? When I started podcasting, these seemed like a foreign concept to me. "Someone pays you money to give them podcast information?" Well, not exactly. There are dedicated sites out there (like the popular Patreon.com) that allow you to collect "member dues" for your podcast. In exchange, you can provide additional content, uncut audio, behind-the-scenes clips, ad-free episodes, etc. The only limit to what you provide to your members is imagination.

Now that I've been podcasting for a while, I've noticed that these membership sites are becoming more common. There are now organizations that will even set up a separate podcast feed for your paid listeners versus the people who can listen anywhere (like Glow.fm). You can have members sign up to be regular contributors to your show, whether they give five, fifty, or even five hundred dollars a month. If you have an audience that's asking you to take them on a deeper journey with you, then this is a great option to monetize your show.

A LITTLE MORE WORK, BUT DEEPER CONNECTION

Unlike the route of affiliate marketing where you have passive income coming in from the affiliate links you share, membership sites can create more work for you. But I wanted to give you some easy ideas to create content for your paid members:

- Monthly Behind-the-Scenes Videos
  - Take them on a tour of your studio, allow them access to behind-the-scenes footage you did with an interview guest that you didn't air (maybe some juicy details that you save for your members).
- Monthly Training Materials
  - If you educate your audience with your podcast, consider creating training material like eBooks, PDFs, videos, etc. to compliment your podcast content and take your audience on a deeper level with you.

COVER YOUR EXPENSES

I've heard podcasters say outright, "Please consider joining our membership community for just $5.00 per month so we can continue to provide you awesome content. This membership fee helps to cover the expenses of this podcast, and in exchange, we do something special for our members each month." Membership sites are a great way to build a community and help support your podcast as it continues to grow.

3.Selling Your Own Services

Are you a coach or consultant, or do you offer any type of service? If so, you can use your podcast as a platform to advertise your services. It's as simple as inserting a self-sponsored ad like, "This episode is sponsored by my _____ services. Go to [insert website] to schedule your consultation today," and then go into detail how that thing can help your listeners. (You already know I'm going to say it, but always be thinking of ways you can *add value* to your audience!)

You could also say something like, "If you're interested in learning more about [insert podcast topic] and going on this journey with me, contact me at [insert e-mail or website]." You have this amazing platform, right? And you've already set it up to be speaking to your ideal listeners about exactly what they want to hear. So why not offer them added value with your services?

4.Selling Merchandise for Your Podcast

Everything I'm about to share with you about selling merchandise is theory. I don't currently sell merchandise for my podcast, but that doesn't mean you shouldn't. If your listeners are asking for something extra or you just want to blast your logo all over some stuff like stickers, sweaters, and mugs, then go for it! But do not—I repeat, *do not*—go into debt or order a ton of inventory simply because you think that's what you're supposed to do. The last thing you want to do is spend a bunch of money on stuff just to have it sit in the bottom of your closet or collect dust in your garage.

Now, that I've given you my "be responsible" speech, I do think merchandise can be a really cool addition to your podcast. It gives you something to give away or sell if you go to a tradeshow or live event. And you can set up an online store to sell your products. Plus, I think it would be pretty cool to see someone wearing a hat or shirt with your podcast logo on it. So, if you feel like this is the monetization route you want to go, by all means explore it and have fun with it! And be sure to share it on social media when your merchandise arrives!

5.Selling Your Own Products, Programs, or Events

This may be the most fun thing ever to talk about. Sure, I love to talk about podcasting in general. But what really fires me up is talking about promoting your own products, programs, live events, etc. on your podcast. It makes me giddy. It makes me talk faster. When someone asks me, "How do you make money podcasting?" this is always the first thing I want to talk about.

But you may not be ready for this step. If you're just starting in the online space or if you don't have an existing business, this *should not* be your first move. It wasn't mine. Sure, I knew deep down that I eventually wanted to create something to sell to my audience, but what? A book? An online course? A live event? I had no clue. But what excited me about creating something on my own to sell was 1) the amount of control I'd have over the creative process of developing something to strategically market to my audience and 2) the fact that there was no cap.

There are endless possibilities for how you can market your product, how many products you can offer your audience, and how often you promote your own stuff. However, there are some ground rules I live by when it comes to selling your own stuff:

1. Don't promote your *paid* products / services / programs / etc. in every episode.
   - Your audience is there for the free content you deliver. Knock their socks off with your free stuff, and they'll be more likely to take interest in your paid offers.
   - My rule of thumb is to talk about paid promotions within episodes once a month. And most of the time, this is more of a subtle mention as opposed to a "Buy this" or "Purchase that" approach! If I'm doing my podcast right, my listeners will know all about how much more value they'd get in one of my paid programs.
   - I never want my audience to feel like I've drawn them into my podcast just to sell them something. I think about those timeshare companies that have gotten a bad reputation of offering you a free meal if you listen to their two-hour sales pitch about their vacation properties all over the world. "No thanks. I'd rather make a PB&J at home." Don't be those people!

2. Make it clear when this offer is expiring.
   - If you're promoting a seasonal offer (like when I talk about my Proffitt Podcasting

course that opens a few times a year), make the dates clear in your episode. You want someone listening to that episode two years from now to know that the offer they're hearing has expired. Otherwise, you'll be dealing with some frustrated "would-be" customers who may not want to buy from you in the future.

3. Be sure that your call-to-action is clear.
   o Are you selling something from your website? Do listeners need to check out another URL? Are you selling something on Amazon that they need to find? Is the link you want them to go to in the show notes?
   o Be very clear about what you want listeners to do.

4. Don't try to sell something to your audience that doesn't make sense for them.
   o I teach podcasting on my podcast. So how awkward would it be if I started a jet-ski company and tried to sell listeners a recreational water vehicle? That doesn't make sense. So, don't try to offer weird things that don't align with your podcast audience.

5. Add value to your audience.
    o   Maybe I should have named this book "Add
        Value to Your Listeners." But I'll say it again:
        add value with your products, programs, or
        events. If at any time you ask yourself, "Am I
        adding value to my audience?" and the
        answer is no, go back to the drawing board.

PRODUCTS, PROGRAMS, AND EVENT IDEAS FOR YOUR PODCAST

We are all about being ethical and showing up with
integrity, always. Likewise, I want you to create a
podcast that has massive success with your audience so
you can build a business that delivers the highest value
to your audience *because you know exactly who they are
and you care about them.* "But I have no idea what I can
create!" may be what you're telling yourself. That's
okay. I have some great ideas for you to explore!

- Digital Products
    o   eBooks
    o   Training videos
    o   Digital planners
    o   Workbooks
    o   Thirty-, sixty-, or ninety-day challenges
- Digital Courses

- ○ Develop a workshop/course that teaches the core principles of your podcast
- Digital Services
  - ○ Provide a "done-for-you" service related to your podcast - different than a consulting service
- Live Events
  - ○ Masterminds
  - ○ Paid membership meetups
  - ○ Conferences related to your podcast

There are so many different things you can do now that you're a podcaster in the online world. And I want you to explore all of the things that you're interested in, but remember that you don't have to do them all! Honestly, I recommend trying out one thing at a time and going from there.

Krystal Proffitt

...there is one key trait that contributes to podcast growth more than anything: consistency!

Chapter 19: Growth Strategies

CHAPTER 19: GROWTH STRATEGIES

Let's pretend you've started and launched your podcast. You're six months to a year into your journey, and you've seen some growth but not enough to really move the needle. What do you do? Well, I want you to take a second and go back to *why* you're doing this podcast in the first place.

Remember Your Why

Did you start this podcast to gain millions of followers? Are you doing this to one day replace your full-time income, with your podcast being the marketing arm for your digital business? Why are you doing this? Why does this podcast matter to you? I want you to take a second to let your answers sink in, because your why will determine how big your podcast gets, how connected your audience feels to you, and how much passion and motivation you'll be able to sustain over the life of your podcast.

Look at the big picture of where this podcast is and where you want it to go. My hope is that you will be consistent with your podcast and your audience will continue to find value in your show.

When Will You Start to See Growth?

If you've recently launched your podcast, there's a good chance you're checking your stats daily. It's natural. Why fight it? I'm not going to tell you to quit, because I did the same thing, and I think it's totally fine. You're looking for validation, right? You're trying to make sure you're on the right track. Nothing wrong with that. But it gets hard to see growth in your podcast if you're checking the stats every single day. Once you've gotten comfortable with only checking your stats a few times a week or even a few times a month, you'll be able to read your data better. You'll see what episodes are resonating, how fast your listenership is growing, and how dispersed your listeners are in your country or around the globe. (That's pretty fantastic in itself!)

What Contributes to Podcast Growth?

Podcast growth depends on many factors, like how frequently you publish. However, there is one key trait that contributes to podcast growth more than anything: consistency! Consistency is key to having a successful podcast. You have to be fully committed to your podcast before you ever even launch. This is incredibly important. And honestly, this is more of a mindset than an actual skill.

Consistency is about commitment. Committing to your podcast. Committing to your audience. Committing to show up every single week.

People need to know *how* to find you and *when* you'll show up again for them. If you don't show up for your audience regularly, they won't know when to show up for you.

YOU NEED DATA TO MEASURE SUCCESS

I was totally prepared to put out at least ten episodes before I decided whether I needed to change things up with my podcast or keep it as is. Some of my initial thoughts were, "Is the music too much? Do I need to switch up my format? Should I prerecord my intro or say it every time?" But you need to create content (and lots of it!) before you start to analyze the success of your show or even individual episodes. You can't measure your podcast growth and stats if you don't have enough info. So, if you're just starting, give yourself a little time (and grace) to start seeing some results before you decide whether what you're doing is working or not.

How Do You Grow?

"Okay, I've done all these things. How do I grow this podcast? How do I scale it? How do I get more downloads? How do I get my podcast in front of more people?" If you've put all of the work in, then the next natural progression of your podcast is growth. Let's talk about some of those ways right now.

Find Other Passionate People in Your Industry

After you've gotten the hang of your podcast, I want you to start finding other passionate people in your industry. What does that mean? Maybe it means industry leaders. Maybe it means people who just love to talk about what your podcast is about. I love it whenever I get around other people that love to talk about podcasting! I totally geek out! So, whenever I start connecting with my fellow podcast enthusiasts, conversations happen that I never would have thought about on my own. I'm able to create new ideas for my audience, and I get more insight to the type of content I should deliver or the things that I should try. I'm also inspired to start trying some of the other strategies that they're experimenting with, whether that's marketing, recording, editing, or anything else. It gives me even more energy to just be around other people who are passionate about podcasting!

I want you not only to find the big players in your industry, but to start networking with other people in your industry. Whether it's in Facebook groups or other online communities or actual in-person events, I want you to get out there. Connect with your audience. Meet other people in your industry. Put yourself out there. Yes, it's uncomfortable at first, but this is a great way to tell people about your podcast and how it's a resource that will help them better their lives or entertain them or make their lives easier or whatever purpose your podcast serves. But you have to get out there and start networking with other people in order for them to know that you're there.

Guesting on Other Podcasts

"What's the fastest way to grow a podcast?" I've heard many experts answer this question the same way: guest on other people's podcasts. You could guest on podcasts related to your industry or ones that have an audience that aligns with yours.

Podcast guesting can be a great collaboration whenever you have two people whose audiences align really well. You'll find it's easy to promote their podcast to your audience and vice versa. It makes everything a lot easier and everyone benefits. Here's how:

- Your audience finds another podcast to listen to once you promote your guest spot.

- Your podcast benefits from the added exposure of your host's audience hearing about what kind of value it can add to their life.
- Your podcast host benefits from filling a slot in their . podcast calendar.
- The host's audience benefits because you're bringing them the amazing value you always deliver to your own audience.

Magic happens when everyone's worlds collide in the right atmosphere with the right intention and purpose.

HOW TO PITCH YOURSELF TO A PODCAST

"How can I approach a podcast about guesting?" There isn't a shortcut to guesting on podcasts. In order to do this properly, you should invest time and energy into how you approach each podcast you'd like to guest on. But here are a few steps to get your brain on the right path:

1. Find podcasts where you ideal listeners will be.
2. Listen to at least one interview episode.
3. Gather valuable information about the podcast.
    - Learn about the host, previous content they've covered, how they conduct their interviews, etc.

4. Identify a few topics you could cover that are related to what your podcast and/or business are about.
5. Pick two to three topics that you'll present to the podcast host and/or their team.
   ○ For example, I could pitch a podcast with the topic, "How to Confidently Start a Podcast with Little Tech Experience."
6. Send them a personalized message with the following information:
   ○ Introduce yourself and your podcast. You could deliver your elevator pitch here.
   ○ Create a personal connection with who they are, what they do, or something that's interesting to grab their attention.
   ○ Offer your potential topic ideas that will deliver value to their audience and be great conversations.
7. Close your message with information on how to contact you, links to previous podcast interviews you've done, and links to your own podcast.

Guesting on podcasts is something you should continue to do throughout the life of your podcast. You may find that it fits into your schedule seasonally or throughout the year, but definitely try to expand the reach of your listener base outside of your current network. This will guarantee that you're getting in front of new, potential listeners.

Guest Posting for Large Publications

Are you great at writing? Or do you feel like you could take some of your previous podcast content and turn it into a stellar blog post? Then I'd urge you to consider pitching yourself to some large online publications. This is something I've personally challenged myself to do more of, and I'll be honest, it's scary. I've been doing my podcast and teaching podcasting for a while now, and I still have thoughts like, "Who am I to write a post for *Forbes* or *Entrepreneur* or any of those other places?" But, you know, sometimes we just have to put ourselves out there and see what happens. And I can't tell you to do it if I'm not doing it myself.

You can use the same steps we just talked about for guesting on podcasts, except you want to make sure you're creating content that's relevant to the publication's target audience. And what's the most important thing to add in? That's right: *value!* It's all about the value.

Don't be afraid to get creative when it comes to growing your podcast. And I will tell you, it does take time to figure out what works and what doesn't. When you start to see some major traction and growth, don't just say, "Oh, that's cool!" See why it's happening. What can you do to replicate those results? How can you do some of the same things to reach even more people? Follow the breadcrumbs of success. Actually, don't just follow—hunt them down like a rabid wolf. It's what I do.

Don't let the fear of looking stupid or thinking that you're not good enough or that no one's actually going to listen to your podcast get in your way...

Chapter 20: Bring It On Home

CHAPTER 20: BRING IT ON HOME

Well, you made it. You've just explored the ways to start, launch, and market your podcast. You now know how to create a podcast your audience will crave. Holy moly, can you believe we're already here? I have to congratulate you. You're doing amazing things, and I cannot wait to see what you create. But I also want to be really real with you before we part ways.

Final Words of Wisdom

I wish I would've had a podcast coach when I started podcasting. Someone to share with me all of the information that's filled these pages. I wish I would've had someone tell me a few things to help me keep going when it got hard. So, I'm sharing those with you now, before I go. Ready?

It's okay that you totally screwed up your thirty-minute solo episode because you were connected to your laptop mic and not your USB mic. Give yourself some grace. It's fine that you forgot to switch your show notes post from "draft" to "published" on your website. It's not the end of the world. It's okay that only half your audience got excited when you shared the piece of content you were most excited to share this month. The people who needed to hear it heard it.

What matters most is that you keep going. Keep giving yourself lots of grace. You're going to mess up. You're going to make mistakes. Take opportunities that scare you a little bit. Step out of your comfort zone, because you never know where those opportunities will take you. Reach out to those big guests. The worst they can say is no.

You can do this. It's scary. It's nerve racking to be vulnerable and put yourself out there. To put your creativity and all of your hard work out into the world, but you can do this. Always put adding value to your audience first and amazing things will happen. I am rooting for you. I am cheering you on. I want to see you succeed.

Don't let the fear of looking stupid or thinking that you're not good enough or that no one's actually going to listen to your podcast get in your way. That's total BS, okay!? I'm just gonna call it what it is. It is BS!

I believe that you have a special message to share, and you're the only one that can tell it the way you tell it. You can do this!"

Remember, keep it up.
We all have to start somewhere!

-Krystal

Invitation to Join Us

If you're looking for an inspiring community of podcasters to help you on your journey, we'd love to have you join us in The Proffitt Podcast Online Community. Head over to:

https://KrystalProffitt.com/podcastcommunity

Resources

There were so many resources, tools, podcast episodes, and other strategies mentioned through the book. For a full clickable list of all the resources organized by chapter and topic, go to

https://KrystalProffitt.com/bookresources

Follow me on your favorite social media platforms:

www.Facebook.com/KrystalProffittTx
www.Instagram.com/KrystalProffittTx
www.YouTube.com/c/KrystalProffitt
www.Pinterest.com/KrystalProffittTx
www.LinkedIn.com/in/krystalproffitt/

Acknowledgements

I want to say thank you so much to the community of podcasters that I've had the privilege of working and connecting with on a deeper level. We've talked so much about value and really understanding your listeners, and I have gone above and beyond - to the *obsessive* level - trying to understand how I can better serve my community. I'm so grateful for every single one of you that have taken the time to meet with me, tell me about your hardships and struggles, and be vulnerable enough to let me help you in a way that has totally blown all of my expectations out of the water.

To all of my students and members of my community, y'all are rock stars! I'm so proud to be your coach and help you along this journey. I can't wait to see where you end up with your podcast and what kind of success you have in the days, weeks, months and years to come.

I have to say a special shout out to the team at Buzzsprout! They have always been so supportive of me and my podcasting journey. I appreciate y'all so much for having an incredible platform that's easy to navigate, and that your mission is to help podcasters succeed! So, thank you so much.

I want to say a special shout out to my friend and mentor, Amy Porterfield. I am so grateful that you took the time to review this book. And for all the incredible knowledge that you have shared on the *Online Marketing Made Easy* Podcast that has helped me tremendously in my online business and becoming a more well-rounded leader. And I'm just so grateful for the opportunity to have worked with you in different ways these past two years!

A huge, huge shout out to my husband, Seth. I am so grateful for all the grace you've given me as I have created different ventures over the last few years. You've been so supportive and you continue to be my biggest cheerleader, my shoulder to cry on, and my ear whenever I just need to talk things out. I'm so extremely proud and grateful of everything that we've been able to accomplish together. So, thank you so much, babe!

To my boys, I hope that you read these words one day. And that you can see your Mama's pretty awesome! And Mama's doing some things that scare her and are putting her out of her comfort zone. But she's doing them anyway. I'm trying my hardest and showing up as the best version of myself while adding value to other people's lives. I hope you see that. And I hope you can appreciate it. Take a little bit of that and apply it to your own lives one day.

To Mom and Dad, what can I say? You've always believed in me. Even when I had crazy ideas or was way too loud in the mornings. You kept telling me to be myself – the silly, truest version of me. And it's the best advice you could've ever given me.

To you, reader, thank you so much for reading this book. I'd love for you to share on social media your biggest takeaways and the number one thing that you loved about this book. Tag me on social media, take a screenshot of the book wherever you're reading and share it. Let me know what you thought. And, as always, ratings and reviews help us content creators so much! So, if you found this book helpful, I'd greatly appreciate you leaving a rating and a review. Share it with your friends, family, or anybody who would be interested in starting a binge worthy podcast.

Start a Binge Worthy Podcast

About the Author

Krystal Proffitt is the host of *The Proffitt Podcast* - where entrepreneurs go to learn how to start, launch, and market their podcasts. She also teaches the basics of content creation, editing, formatting, marketing, and other skills through her digital courses, membership, and YouTube channel dedicated to podcasting.

She lives in Texas with her husband (Seth), their three sons, and snorting Boston Terrier, Wall-E.